I am dedicating this book to all the curvy women out there who are constantly calorie counting. Remember, no man likes to chew on bones!

The Italian Diet

THE
ITALIAN
DIET

GINO D'ACAMPO

Over 100 healthy Italian recipes to help
you lose weight and love food

INTRODUCTION BY JULIETTE KELLOW, BSC RD
PHOTOGRAPHY BY KATE WHITAKER

KYLE BOOKS

Acknowledgments

Although Italian cuisine is actually generally really healthy, this book was still quite a challenge for me, so I need to say a big thank you to all my family, especially my wife Jessie and my boys Luciano and Rocco, for putting up with me disappearing for many days over the last few months to research various recipes!

Once again, a big thank you to all the crew at Kyle Cathie, who trusted me to write their third book, especially to Kyle, Sophie, and Kate!

To everybody at Bonta Italia, Marco, Lina, Franco, and Loredana. The continuous support you show me is very much appreciated—*Grazie*!

A special thank you to Juliette, Nicole, and Ali, who tried and tested my recipes—here's to calorie counting!

As always, the last shout out has to go to the "Don," Mr. Jeremy Hicks... You are simply the best!

Grazie to all of you for once again choosing my book—*Buon Appetito* !

www.ginodacampo.com

Photographic acknowledgments

page 33: Italian actress Maria-Grazia Cucinotta; Ferdinando Scianna/Magnum Photos
Page 45: *Pane, Amore e Fantasia;* Gala/S.G.C./Titanus/The Kobal Collection
Page 61: *Roman Holiday;* Paramount/The Kobal Collection
Page 77: *Le due vite di Mattia Pascal;* Excelsior/Cinecitta/Antenne 2/The Kobal Collection
Page 99: Italian actress Claudia Cardinale; Universal/The Kobal Collection
Page 127: *Stromboli;* Berit Films/The Kobal Collection/Poletto, G.B.
Page 145: *La Mortadella;* Warner Bros./The Kobal Collection/Secchiaroli, Tazio
Page 167: *La Dolce Vita;* Riama-Patha/The Kobal Collection
Page 179: *La Grande Bouffe;* Mara/Capitolina/The Kobal Collection

Important notes

All recipe analysis is per portion.

Published in 2010 by Kyle Books,
an imprint of Kyle Cathie Limited
www.kylebooks.com

ISBN: 978-1-906868-21-5

A catalog record for this title is available from the Library of Congress

10 9 8 7 6 5 4 3 2 1

Text copyright © 2010 by Gino D'Acampo and Juliette Kellow
Photographs copyright © 2010 by Kate Whitaker
Design copyright © 2010 by Kyle Cathie Limited

Design Nicky Collings
Photography Kate Whitaker
Project editor Sophie Allen
Food stylist Nicole Herft
Props stylist Wei Tang
Americanizer Margaret Parrish
Copy editor Stephanie Evans
Proofreader Ruth Baldwin
Indexer Alex Corrin
Production Gemma John

Color reproduction by Sang Choy
Printed and bound in Singapore by Craft Print International Ltd.

The information and advice contained in this book are intended as a general guide to dieting and healthy eating and are not specific to individuals or their particular circumstances. This book is not intended to replace treatment by a qualified health care practitioner. Neither the authors nor the publishers can be held responsible for claims arising from the inappropriate use of any dietary regime. Do not attempt self-diagnosis or self-treatment for serious or long-term conditions without consulting a medical professoinal or qualified practitoner.

Contents

WELCOME TO THE ITALIAN DIET

After the success of my first two books, *Fantastico!* and *Buonissimo!*, it would have been very easy for me to write a similar Italian cookbook. However, I started to wonder—why not challenge myself by writing a book that would help people reduce their calorie intake but not compromise on flavors? Rather than focus on typical diet ingredients, low-fat ready meals, and restrained eating, I wanted this book to be a celebration of food.

Before I started writing, I did a lot of research on what kind of diet/healthy cookbooks are available and, to my surprise, there are many books around, but often with boring recipes in them. Even more surprising was that none of them really concentrated on healthy Italian meals. There is a misconception that pasta, cheeses, and desserts are a sin in the diet world, but, of course, this is not the truth. Italians love their food and *The Italian Diet* will definitely make everyone feel slimmer and healthier. This is pretty much proven by looking at the Italian population—they are one of the slimmest nations in Europe, are less likely to die from cancer or heart disease, and they enjoy a greater longevity of life than most other Europeans. Remember: anything in moderation is good for you.

In *The Italian Diet* you will find recipes that are easy to prepare and full of flavors, but you will not feel that you are calorie counting. I have also thought about many of you who regularly entertain or cook for your families, who don't need to calorie count, and, I promise you, no one will ever be able to taste the difference. For this book, I have continued to use simple ingredients that require very little cooking, so my motto, as always, still stands...

Minimum Effort, Maximum Satisfaction!

Enjoy and *Buon Appetito!*

INTRODUCTION BY JULIETTE KELLOW, BSc RD

Want to lose weight without giving up all the foods you love? Or do you simply wish you could eat healthily without feeling pressured to fill up on cottage cheese and carrot juice? Then congratulations on picking up this book! *The Italian Diet* is ideal if you want to shift those stubborn extra pounds but love food and can't bear the thought of feeling hungry or deprived. It's also perfect if you simply want to put the joy back into healthy eating.

Based on the Italian way of eating, this is a diet book like no other. You won't find lists of foods to avoid or need to go in search of weird and wonderful diet ingredients you've never heard of. Instead, you'll find the pages packed with familiar, fresh, and delicious foods that are typically eaten as part of a traditional Italian diet.

Opting to eat like an Italian may not seem like the obvious choice when you want to lose weight or eat healthily. After all, Italian dishes come in huge portions and are packed with calories and fat, right? Actually, wrong! Many of us think that typical Italian food consists of doughy, deep-crust pizzas loaded with meat and cheese, cream-laden pasta sauces, large platefuls of fatty meat, and bowlfuls of tiramisu. In fact, meals served up in traditional Italian homes and trattorias are nothing like this: instead, ingredients tend to be fresh and portions small. Vegetables are an important part of meals, herbs and garlic are used to flavor food, wine and water is on the table, and fruit is eaten for dessert. In reality, a true Italian diet is an extremely healthy way of eating, so it can help us to keep well, get slim—and stay that way.

The Italians are living proof that it works, too. People living in Italy are among the slimmest in Europe and are far less likely to be overweight or obese than people in the US. They also live longer and are less likely to die from cancer or heart disease. What's more, they manage to achieve this without constant dieting. But perhaps the best news is that Italians enjoy good health and slim bodies while still savoring delicious food they actually want to eat.

If you love life as well as great food, this is the book for you. We believe that when you start *The Italian Diet*, you will quickly look and feel slimmer, fitter, and healthier. And once you've discovered and enjoyed this new way of eating, you'll want to follow it forever!

WHY THIS DIET?

This is a diet you will actually want to follow. Here's why:

- It's about pleasure—you'll find you enjoy every part of the meal process from shopping for the ingredients through to preparing dishes and enjoying them with your family and friends.
- It's based on a traditional Italian diet, which is incredibly healthy and packed with nutritious foods.
- It uses fresh ingredients that are in season, so food tastes fantastic—this means you won't need to add lots of fat, salt, or sugar to give flavor.
- Meals are simple and easy to prepare and use foods you can buy in your local supermarket, farmers' market, or from your butcher, grocer, and fishmonger. You won't need to go to health food stores or track down special ingredients.
- No foods are banned—you can still enjoy pasta, bread, and desserts and have an appetizer and a main course.
- You can indulge in a glass of wine with meals.

WEIGHING UP THE FACTS

If you're in any doubt about how filling up on delicious Italian food can help you stay slim and healthy, it's worth taking a look at some facts and figures. According to scientific studies, Italians are among the slimmest people in Europe. By contrast, according to the Centers for Disease Control and Prevention, a massive 67 percent of adults in the US are overweight or obese, which makes the US one of the fattest nations in the world. In comparison, 40 percent of Italian adults are overweight or obese, giving Italy the second lowest incidence of overweight and obesity in Europe. Just over a third of American adults—34 percent—are obese, compared to just 8 percent of Italians. In fact, of the 27 countries in the European Union, Italy has the lowest rate of obesity. It's perhaps no surprise, then, that the average Body Mass Index (BMI) is much lower for Italians than for Americans as well. In the US, the average BMI among adults is 29. Compare this with Italians, whose average BMI for men is 25.4 and for women 24.1.

Better still, Italians are far less hung up on dieting—and when they do actually try to lose weight, they are generally fairly successful at it. According to the *Cuisine Study* carried out by global market research company GfK in 2005, just 26 percent of Italian women had started a diet in the previous two years. Of these women, 34 percent lost all the weight they set out to lose or more. By comparison, a survey by *Self* magazine, conducted in partnership with the University of North Carolina, Chapel Hill found that 67 percent of American women were trying to lose weight, with varying degress of success.

DO I NEED TO LOSE WEIGHT?

Health experts around the world use a scale called the Body Mass Index (BMI) to help identify whether a person needs to lose weight. This measurement looks at the suitability of a person's weight for their height. It's relatively easy to calculate your BMI if you have a calculator and know your weight in pounds and your height in inches. All you need to do is divide your weight by your height squared and multiple by 703, then compare it to guidelines. For example, if you weigh 165lb and are 5'5" (65 inches) tall, the calculation is as follows: [165 ÷ (65)2] x 703 = 27.45, which means you are overweight. Alternatively, you can log on to the Centers for Disease Control and Prevention website **www.cdc.gov/healthyweight/assessing/bmi/** and use its calculator.

As a general rule, the higher your BMI, the greater your risk of health problems, such as heart disease, stroke, high blood pressure, type 2 diabetes, certain cancers, and a reduced life expectancy.

BODY MASS INDEX

BMI	CATEGORY
Less than 18.5	Underweight
18.5 to 24.9	Normal weight
25 to 29.9	Overweight
30 to 39.9	Obese
40 or more	Morbidly obese

Italians have the lowest rate of obesity in the European Union

LA DOLCE VITA

Italians aren't just slimmer than Americans, they also live longer. In fact, Italians enjoy an extra two years of life! According to data from the Central Intelligence Agency in the US, the average life expectancy for Italians is 80.33 years. Among Americans, the average life expectancy is 78.24 years. Meanwhile, Italy has a more aged population than the US, with 26 percent of the Italian population being over 60.

As for heart disease and cancer, when age is considered—bearing in mind that there is a large elderly population living in Italy—figures from a report in 2008 called *European Cardiovascular Disease Statistics* reveal that Italians are less likely to die from cancer and heart problems such as coronary heart disease and stroke than most other Europeans. The key, experts agree, is a healthy diet and lifestyle.

PASTA PERFECTION

When it comes to Italian beauties, there's no one more famous than the actress Sophia Loren. More than 1,500 people in an online poll voted her, at the age of 71, the world's most naturally beautiful woman, ahead of celebrity beauties less than half her age. When asked for her secrets, Sophia simply claimed her youthful looks were down to a love of life, spaghetti, and the odd bath in olive oil! "Everything you see, I owe to spaghetti!" she famously said. In her book *Women & Beauty* she states, "Italians are lucky to live with a culinary heritage that relies on pasta because it is a complex carbohydrate and a very efficient and healthy fuel for the body." Wise words from a beautiful lady.

A TASTE OF THE MED

One of the main reasons Italian people tend to remain slim and healthy is thought to be their diet. In many parts of the country, families still eat a traditional Mediterranean-style diet—a collection of eating habits that are followed by people living in the countries that border the Mediterranean Sea.

As far back as the 1950s, experts began to recognize that people living in Mediterranean countries tended to have healthier hearts and lower rates of heart disease. In 1958, American scientist Professor Ancel Keys began the *Seven Countries Study*, a groundbreaking piece of research that studied the diets, lifestyle, and incidence of coronary heart disease in almost 13,000 middle-aged men from seven countries for 10 years. His findings highlighted that in those countries where intakes of saturated fats were high, such as the United States and Finland, so, too, was the incidence of coronary heart disease. In contrast, the disease was far less common in countries like Greece and the southern part of Italy, where saturated fat intakes were lower.

Fifty years on, research increasingly reveals many other potential health benefits, too. In 2008, Italian researchers looked at 12 international studies that tracked the dietary habits and health of more than 1.5 million people. Those people who had strictly stuck to a Mediterranean diet were found to have a 9 percent drop in both overall mortality and death from heart disease, but also a 6 percent reduction in cancer and a 13 percent drop in Parkinson's and Alzheimer's disease. Meanwhile, other recent research published in the *British Medical Journal* found that closely following a Med-style diet was linked to a large reduction in the risk of developing type 2 diabetes. There's also evidence that a Med-style diet can help people to lose weight more effectively than a low-fat diet. A recent study in the *New England Journal of Medicine* found that a Mediterranean diet resulted in greater weight loss than a low-fat diet, even though both provided the same number of calories.

So what exactly do people eat in Mediterranean countries? It's well established among health professionals that traditional eating habits in this region match many of the healthy eating guidelines. Portion sizes tend to be quite small and diets include lots of fresh, natural foods, and few processed ones. Fruit, vegetables, bread, pasta, rice, beans, and nuts form the main part of the diet and fish tends to be eaten in good amounts, usually in preference to meat. Olive oil is the main fat consumed, and is used in cooking and as a salad dressing. Although salt is still added to dishes, herbs, garlic, and black pepper are used to add flavor. And small amounts of red wine are consumed with meals. Meat, eggs, and full-fat dairy products are usually eaten only in small amounts.

BUON APPETITO

Italy sits in the heart of the Mediterranean and so, unsurprisingly, most Italians eat a traditional diet. There's little reliance on prepackaged meals or takeout. Instead, meals tend to be based on fresh ingredients. And, according to GfK's *Cuisine Study*, 90 percent of Italians cook every day. There's no age barrier either—young or old, 9 out of 10 Italians prepare their own food from scratch on a daily basis! Most Italians stock their kitchens with a few simple essentials and then add to these with fresh ingredients that they buy daily from local markets and supermarkets. This means most meals tend to be based on seasonal ingredients that are produced locally. And the real secret, most Italian mammas will tell you, is to buy the best-quality ingredients you can afford—that way you're guaranteed a meal that's packed with flavor.

MUST-HAVE ITALIAN INGREDIENTS

OLIVE OIL

With so many olive oils available, it can be difficult to know which one to choose. But as a golden rule, the more you pay, the better the taste, so buy the best you can afford. Extra-virgin olive oil is made from the first pressing of the olives and has a deep green color, a low acidity, and a strong flavor, which means you get plenty of taste even when you use just a small amount. Heating impairs the flavor and aroma, however, so don't waste it by cooking with it. Instead, it's best to use it for dressings, dipping, and to drizzle over finished dishes.

Virgin olive oil is more acidic and can be used in the same way as extra-virgin varieties but it's also suitable for cooking. Pure olive oil is a mixture of virgin and refined olive oils and is the best one for cooking, since it's more stable at higher temperatures. However, it has the least flavor. Like all oils, olive oil is high in fat— 1 tablespoonful contains 11g of fat. That said, the type of fat it contains is predominantly heart-healthy monounsaturated fat, which research shows lowers "bad" or LDL cholesterol, while maintaining levels of "good" or HDL cholesterol. This is welcome news, since abnormal cholesterol levels increase the risk of heart disease. And there's more: olive oil is a rich source of vitamin E and polyphenols, both of which act as antioxidants and so are important for a healthy heart.

There's no denying olive oil is also high in calories—100 calories per tablespoon—so if you want to lose weight, it's best to use small amounts. However, there is some evidence that olive oil may help us to lose weight. In one very small study, in which overweight or obese men ate a diet rich in monounsaturated fat, they lost more weight and fat than those eating a diet rich in saturated fat,

While low-carb diets may have been popular in recent years, health experts have always recommended eating starchy, fiber-rich carbs as part of a healthy balanced diet. According to the US Department of Agriculture, at least 3oz of starchy carbohydrates such as whole-wheat bread, whole-wheat cereals, pasta, and rice should eaten daily—and that's exactly how most Italians eat: pasta, rice, potatoes, and polenta tend to form the base of most meals in Italy—and bread is usually on the table. Pasta is an especially good choice if you're trying to lose weight, since it has a low glycemic index and so is good for filling you up and keeping you satisfied. Take care not to overcook it though, since *al dente* (firm to the bite) pasta has a lower glycemic index (GI; see opposite) than soft pasta because the digestive process takes longer to break down the starch into sugars, slowing the release of these sugars into the bloodstream.

even though both diets provided a similar number of calories. And in a separate laboratory study, olive oil has been shown to help break down fats. More research is needed, but these findings could, in part, help to explain why Italians tend to be slimmer than other Europeans and Americans.

PASTA

There's more to Italian pasta than spaghetti, lasagne, and tagliatelle. Italian kitchens tend to be stocked with a variety of shapes and sizes, such as fettuccine, fusilli, rigatoni, angel hair (capellini), orzo, farfalle, maccheroni, orecchiette, and linguine. The type of pasta you buy may not seem important, but Italian mammas will tell you it's vital to match the correct pasta to the correct sauce. Fine, delicate pastas such as angel hair are best with light tomato sauces, while heavier tube pastas such as penne or rigatoni work better with chunkier meaty sauces that coat the pasta on both the inside and outside.

PULSES

Ingredients such as chick peas, cannellini beans, cranberry beans, and lentils are often included in home-cooked Italian dishes such as soups and hearty stews. There's no need to use dried varieties—canned are just as good and need no preparation other than opening the can, but do choose those without added salt. In addition to containing a variety of nutrients, including iron, calcium, and zinc, pulses are all low in fat but packed with protein and fiber and have a low GI, making them the perfect food for dieters. In fact, scientific research increasingly shows that protein and fiber is the perfect hunger-fighting combo. What's more, pulses are also packed with soluble fiber, which research shows can help to maintain blood sugar levels and reduce cholesterol.

THE GLYCEMIC INDEX EXPLAINED

The glycemic index (GI) looks at the impact carbohydrate-containing foods have on our blood sugar levels. Foods with a low-GI value slowly release sugar into the blood, providing a steady supply of energy, leaving us feeling satisfied for longer, and therefore less likely to snack. In contrast, foods with a high-GI value cause a rapid—but short-lived—rise in blood sugar. This quickly leaves us lacking in energy and feeling hungry, so we're more likely to snack. Over time, this frequent snacking may lead to weight gain. Health experts recommend we opt as often as possible for carbohydrate-rich foods with a low to moderate GI, since they help to keep us fuller for longer. Examples of foods with a low GI include vegetables, pasta, beans, lentils, barley, oats, nuts, yogurt, apples, pears, peaches, oranges, and grapes. Foods with a high GI include white bread, potatoes, white rice, candy, and some sugary cereals.

TOMATOES

Whether fresh, canned, puréed, or sieved (passata), tomatoes are an essential ingredient in Italian cooking. All varieties contribute to our five fruit and veg a day (see page 16), are low in fat and calories—one fresh tomato contains just 15 calories—and provide fiber to help add bulk to our diet so that we feel fuller for longer. They are also a good source of vitamin C and an antioxidant called lycopene, which research shows may reduce the risk of heart disease and several types of cancer, especially prostrate cancer, and may help to protect the skin from the harmful effects of ultraviolet light. Better still, you don't need to rely on fresh tomatoes to get these benefits—in fact, cooked and processed tomatoes provide a more concentrated and better absorbed source of lycopene than fresh ones! Cooked tomatoes tend to have a stronger flavor than raw ones, so you won't need to add as much salt to dishes when you use them, and their naturally occurring sugars add sweetness. (Avoid cooking tomato-based dishes in aluminum pans, however, since the acid they contain can interact with the metal, leaving an unpleasant taste.) And here's another tip: when using fresh tomatoes in cold dishes like salads, make sure they are fully ripe and allow them to reach room temperature before serving them, since they'll have a much better flavor.

ONIONS

Onions are included in most Italian dishes and are added liberally to sauces, soups, and meat dishes. But when it comes to flavor, Italians know their onions. As a rule, small round onions usually have the strongest flavor and smell and so are best for cooking, whereas red and large onions tend to be sweeter and milder, so are a good choice for eating raw. Shallots and scallions also have a mild, delicate flavor. Onions are low in calories and fat, count toward our five-a-day, and are a source of fiber. Moreover, they contain phytochemicals, such as quercetin, which acts as an antioxidant and have been linked to keeping our heart healthy, lowering the risk of cancer, helping to lessen the pain associated with conditions like arthritis and even easing the symptoms of allergies like hayfever.

Meanwhile, research has shown that a regular intake of onions may help to lower blood sugar levels, thanks to the sulfur compounds they contain. These compounds appear to boost levels of insulin, a hormone that helps to mop up sugar

THE ITALIAN WAY TO FIVE-A-DAY

Italians eat, on average, a whopping 817g of vegetables a day—higher than the minimum recommendation. It's something they've been doing for many years, too—the average intake of fruits and vegetables has changed little since 1970. Fruits and vegetables are low in fat and calories but high in filling fiber, so they are an important part of a healthy weight-loss plan. They also contain phytochemicals with their important antioxidant properties, good intakes of which help to protect against a variety of diseases, including heart disease and cancer. This is why health experts recommend eating five portions every day. Italians have little trouble eating this amount and will usually eat far more! Popular vegetables include tomatoes, garlic, onions, artichokes, peppers, eggplant, fennel, mushrooms, cabbage, zucchini, celery, asparagus, broccoli, and spinach, which are typically added to pasta, risottos, pizza, and soup or turned into salads, antipasti, or side dishes. Fruits such as oranges, figs, pears, cherries, grapes, berries, plums, melons, and apples are eaten between meals and as an alternative to heavy desserts.

What counts as a portion of fruit and vegetable?

A portion of fruit or vegetables should weigh at least 3oz. All fruits and vegetables count, including fresh, frozen, canned, and dried, as well as pure juices. The following all count as one serving:

- 1 tomato, 7 cherry tomatoes, or 1 heaping tablespoon of tomato paste
- 3 heaping tablespoons of vegetables, beans, or lentils
- a cereal bowl of salad
- ½ avocado
- 1 apple, pear, orange, peach, or nectarine
- 2 plums, satsumas, or kiwi fruit
- 1 large slice of melon or fresh pineapple
- a handful of grapes
- 7 strawberries, 14 cherries, or 20 raspberries
- 3 fresh d apricots
- 3 heaping tablespoons of fruit salad or stewed fruit
- 1 heaping tablespoon of dark or golden raisins
- 1 small glass (½ cup) fruit juice or fruit smoothie

TOP TIPS

- Potatoes don't count toward the five-a-day because they're a starchy food and don't contain the same nutrients as fruits and veggies.
- Juice counts as only one serving no matter how much you have because it doesn't contain much fiber and the juicing process "squashes" the natural sugars out of the fruit cells, which can harm teeth if consumed frequently.
- Dried beans and pulses count as only one serving no matter how much you have because they contain different nutrients from most other fruits and vegetables.

in the blood and take it to the cells where it's needed to provide energy. This, in turn, helps to lower blood sugar. If you want to guarantee lots of these phytochemicals, go for the most pungent onions—if they make your eyes water when you cut them, chances are they'll have the most antioxidants!

FRESH GARLIC

Known for its unmistakable smell and taste, garlic is great for adding flavor to dishes so that you can cut down on salt. Garlic is used liberally in most Italian meals including sauces, dressings, pasta, pizzas, and some risottos. A compound called allicin is responsible for garlic's characteristic flavor and also for its many health benefits, which are thought to include reducing the risk of heart attacks, high blood pressure, and certain cancers. Garlic has been shown to have antibacterial and anti-inflammatory properties, too. Allicin is released when garlic is chopped or crushed, and the more finely it's chopped, the stronger the taste of the dish will be. It's also worth knowing that the flavor can take several minutes to develop, so for the best taste in dishes, add garlic at least 5 minutes before the end of cooking.

DRIED PORCINI MUSHROOMS

These pantry cupboard standbys add a delicious, concentrated mushroom flavor to risottos, soups, and casseroles. This means you don't need to use as much salt in dishes. Dried porcini mushrooms need to be covered in a little boiling water and left to soak for about 15 minutes to reconstitute them. Then drain them—reserving the liquid, which can be strained and used in place of some of the stock—and chop. When opening the package, you should get a strong mushroom aroma—if there's no smell, there will be little taste.

GOODNESS IN A NUTSHELL

Italians love to eat nuts and this is good for promoting healthy hearts and trim waistlines. Most dieters avoid nuts because of their high calorie content. However, some studies suggest that small amounts of nuts may aid weight loss when eaten as part of a healthy diet that includes moderate amounts of fat (rather than one that's low in fat). This may be because people find it easier to stick to a diet with fewer restrictions. But nuts also contain the perfect hunger-fighting combination of protein and fiber: snacking on them may help to keep us fuller for longer so we take in fewer calories overall. The conclusion of many studies is that frequently eating nuts lowers the risk of heart disease. While most of the heart health benefits are probably linked to the monounsaturated and polyunsaturated fats they contain, nuts are also a source of antioxidants such as vitamin E and selenium, both of which may help to protect against heart disease. Finally, other research has linked nuts with a lower risk of developing type 2 diabetes, possibly because the fiber and magnesium they contain help to keep blood sugar and insulin levels steady.

Antioxidants are natural substances found in certain foods—mostly fruits, vegetables, and whole grains—that help to combat the effects of potentially harmful molecules called free radicals. These free radicals are created naturally as a side effect of metabolism, but levels can increase dramatically when we are exposed to health baddies such as cigarette smoke or pollution. This is bad news because free radicals have the potential to damage cells, increasing the risk of health problems such as heart disease and cancer. That's why it's important to eat plenty of foods that contain antioxidants. Quite simply, the more antioxidants we have in our diet, the more potential we have to fight harmful free radicals and the less likely we are to suffer damage that can leave us with health problems.

LEMONS

Both the juice and zest of lemons add flavor to many Italian dishes, including antipasti, salad dressings, fish dishes, and marinades for meat. Better still, the tartness of these citrus fruits helps to reduce the amount of salt needed in cooking. To get the most juice from fresh lemons, make sure they are at room temperature and roll them gently between your palms before squeezing. Buy unwaxed fruits if you're going to be using the zest and avoid the pith—it will make dishes taste bitter. Meanwhile, although it's virtually free of calories, lemon juice is rich in antioxidant vitamin C—just 1 tablespoon provides 10 percent of the recommended daily amount of this nutrient. Plus citrus fruits also contain compounds called limonoids that may help to fight cancer.

Even though wine tends to be consumed with most meals, Italians generally drink in moderation. According to the most recent European Cardiovascular Disease Statistics report, Italians drink 2.75 gallons of pure alcohol per year, which translates into about 20 units of alcohol a week. The World Health Organization figures show an even smaller rate of consumption, with Italians drinking 2.1 gallons of pure alcohol per year (the equivalent of 15 units a week).

Whether the health benefits of alcohol outweigh the risks continues to be debated. It's widely accepted that drinking excessively increases the risk of liver disease, high blood pressure, and cancers of the mouth, throat, esophagus, colon, and breast. Plus, alcohol is packed with calories and so can contribute to obesity. However, there is some evidence that small amounts of alcohol can help boost our health. In particular, our hearts appear to love an occasional sip. Alcohol in moderation has been shown to boost levels of HDL or "good" cholesterol (which protects against heart disease) and reduce the stickiness of blood, so helping to prevent blood clots that can cause heart attacks or strokes.

It's not just red wine that has health benefits, however. Studies show that small amounts of any alcohol can help to keep the heart healthy, especially when it's drunk with meals, rather than alone. But before popping that cork, be forewarned. The key word is "moderation," and that means just one or two units of alcohol a day. And sadly, when it comes to protecting against heart disease, the health benefits kick in only for men over the age of 40 and postmenopausal women.

RICE

Although Italians don't eat as much rice as many other nations, this grain is a key ingredient in one of the country's signature dishes—risotto. In fact, Italy is the leading producer of rice in Europe, particularly cultivating superfine varieties such as Arborio and Carnaroli, which are used to make risotto. In fact, this dish is so popular in certain parts of the country that there's even a famous Italian saying, "Rice is born in water but dies in wine," which refers to the fact that the first liquid to be added to a risotto is wine. Although less nutritious than brown rice, risotto rice still contains starchy carbs to provide us with energy—and once cooked it has a soft, creamy texture that seems really indulgent, so that you will feel satisfied after a small portion.

RED AND WHITE WINE

Wine is an essential ingredient in Italy. It's added to pasta sauces, risottos, stews, soups, and desserts. Wine gives a rich flavor to dishes—the alcohol evaporates during cooking, leaving behind a delicious taste without all the calories. For example, only 10 percent of the alcohol will remain in a casserole that's simmered for two hours. It's important to use a good-quality wine in cooking, not the dregs in a bottle that has been hanging around for days—the rule of thumb is: if you don't want to drink it, don't cook with it. In health terms, red wine is packed with antioxidants that are known to protect against heart disease. In particular, the skins of red grapes contain resveratrol, a naturally occurring flavonoid that appears to offer greater antioxidant benefits than better-known antioxidants like vitamins C and E.

HOW MUCH CAN I SAFELY DRINK?

It is recommended that men drink no more than 3–4 units of alcohol a day, and women no more than 2–3 units daily. The number of units in a drink depends on the bottle or glass size and how strong the drink is. It's not as simple as assuming one drink equals one unit—one drink alone may provide all your daily units.

Here's a guideline:

DRINK	QUANTITY	NUMBER OF UNITS	CALORIES
Single measure of spirits	25ml	1	50
Large single measure of spirits	35ml	1.5	75
Glass of sherry or port	50ml	1	75
Bottle of wine cooler	275ml	1–1.5	200
Glass of champagne	125ml	1.5	100
Small glass of wine	125ml	1.5	100
Standard glass of wine	175ml	2	130
Large glass of wine	250ml	3	200
Ordinary-strength beer, ale, or cider	1 pint	2	200
Strong stout or cider	1 pint	3	250

PARMESAN CHEESE

This strong, tasty cheese—also known as Parmigiano Reggiano—is an essential ingredient in Italian kitchens. It is used to top pasta dishes and soups and is added to creamy sauces and risottos. Like all hard cheeses, Parmesan is relatively high in calories and fat, but it still contains 5 percent fewer calories and 18 percent less fat than Cheddar. Add to this the fact that only small amounts are needed because it has such a robust flavor. It's clear Parmesan is actually a better choice if you want to lose weight. Meanwhile, Parmesan contains almost a third more calcium per 3½oz than Cheddar. This is great news, since this bone-building mineral has also been found to help burn fat, particularly from around our waistlines. With the exception of mascarpone, most other popular Italian cheeses have a lower calorie and fat content than Cheddar, with some, notably mozzarella and ricotta, actually being great choices for dieters.

OLIVES

Olives are great for nibbling on and make a healthier and lower-calorie alternative to fat-laden potato chips and crackers—each olive contains just 3 calories. But they're also a popular addition to many Italian dishes, including pizzas, salads, pasta sauces, and meat dishes. The difference between green and black olives is their degree of ripeness—green olives are unripe and so are denser and have a more bitter flavor than black olives, which are fully ripe. Popular Italian olive varieties include Liguria, Ponentine, Gaeta, and Lugano—all of which are black. Unsurprisingly, olives contain similar nutrients to olive oil. They're a good source of monounsaturated fats and contain vitamin E and polyphenols. Olives are usually high in salt, though, so if you're cooking with them, you won't need to add much extra salt to the dish. Also, olives can become bitter if they are cooked for too long, so it's best to add them to hot dishes toward the end of cooking.

SMILE AND SAY CHEESE...

Cheddar contains 410cal and 34g fat per 3½oz. Here's how some of the most popular Italian cheeses compare (all values are per 3½oz):

Mascarpone	425cal	43g fat
Pecorino	390cal	33g fat
Fontina	390cal	31g fat
Parmesan	390cal	28g fat
Provolone	350cal	27g fat
Gorgonzola	320cal	27g fat
Mozzarella	260cal	20g fat
Ricotta	145cal	11g fat

BALSAMIC VINEGAR

This rich, slightly sweet vinegar is a must for most Italian dressings but is also the perfect partner for fruits such as strawberries, since it helps to bring out their flavor. Just like wine, the longer the vinegar has been aged, the better the quality and the more expensive it tends to be. To guarantee the real thing, look on the label for the words *aceto balsamico tradizionale di Modena*—meaning that it's been produced according to the traditional methods. Fortunately, only small amounts of balsamic vinegar are needed to give a good flavor and it lasts indefinitely, so there's no pressure to use it up quickly—simply keep it in a cool, dark pantry away from heat. Finally, as with tomatoes, avoid using it in aluminum pans, since the acid in the vinegar can react with the metal and taint the flavor of a dish.

FRESH HERBS

No good Italian kitchen is without a selection of fresh herbs. While it's easy to buy fresh herbs these days, it's more economical to grow your own in the garden, on a windowsill, or even in pots in the kitchen. You won't go wrong if you have a ready supply of basil, oregano, parsley, rosemary, and mint on hand. It's particularly important to use leafy herbs like basil, parsley, and mint when they're fresh—their flavor deteriorates in the drying process. Too much heating also destroys the flavor of fresh herbs, so add them toward the end of cooking. Herbs with woody stems, like thyme, oregano, and bay, keep their flavor when dried, so if you don't have fresh ones on hand, using dried varieties won't make a massive difference to the flavor of your finished dish. As a guide, 1 tablespoon of fresh herbs is the equivalent of 1 teaspoon of dried herbs.

SEAFOOD... AND EAT IT!

Fish forms an integral part of the Italian diet. According to a recent European Union Seafood Industry Report, on average, in 2005, Italians ate 55lb of seafood per person per year—roughly 3.5 portions a week. Health experts recognize that fish is an important part of a healthy diet. In fact, the common recommendation is that we eat two servings of fish every week, one of which should be an oil-rich fish such as sardines, pilchards, fresh tuna, whitebait, anchovies, mackerel, herrings, salmon, or trout.

All fish contains protein, which helps to keep us fuller for longer—good news when we are trying to lose weight. Better still, white fish is low in fat, reasonably low in calories, and contains several B vitamins—species popular in Italy include sea bass, red mullet, sea bream, sole, hake, halibut, and cod. Oil-rich fish are higher in fat than white fish, but that fat is the heart-healthy omega-3 fat, which helps to keep the heart beating regularly, protects the small arteries that carry blood to the heart from damage, helps to lower levels of triglycerides (a type of blood fat), and makes blood less sticky, so, in turn, preventing blood clots from forming. Research also shows that eating more omega-3 fats can help to improve the chances of survival after a heart attack. What's more, oil-rich fish are an important source of vitamins A and D and a range of B vitamins. Shellfish such as shrimp, mussels, clams, crabs, lobsters, medallions, and langoustines are also eaten frequently in Italy and these can help to add to levels of nutrients such as selenium, zinc, iodine, and copper.

GET ACTIVE

While enjoying an Italian-style diet will help to shift those stubborn pounds, you'll have even more success—and find you shape up more quickly—if you also do more exercise. The good news is that this doesn't mean you have to join a gym or jog for hours on end. In Italy, people tend to be more active in their normal, everyday lives. For example, in many parts of Italy, people still enjoy *la passeggiata*—an evening stroll—before going home to prepare dinner. It might not burn as many calories as an aerobics class, but it's certainly a better option than lounging in front of the television and can help us on our way to achieving 10,000 steps each day—the recommended amount for good health.

Health experts advocate 30 minutes of moderate-intensity activity at least five times a week. But if we want to lose weight, we should increase this to 45 minutes to an hour each day. Good options include brisk walking, cycling, swimming, and dancing. It's fine to break your daily activity up into chunks, too, such as four 15-minute walks in a day. Check out how many calories different activities burn in the chart on the following page.

CALORIE BURNERS!

ACTIVITY	CALORIES BURNED IN 30 MINUTES
Preparing and cooking meals	87
Shopping for groceries	93
Sex	105
Washing the car	116
Brisk walking	122
Housework	122
Slow cycling	140
Playing with children	140
Gardening	159
Aerobics class	210
Fast dancing	210
Swimming	210
Cardiovascular gym workout	274
Martial arts, such as judo, karate, and kick boxing	318

CALORIE VALUES ARE BASED ON A PERSON WEIGHING 155 POUNDS.

GUIDELINE DAILY AMOUNTS FOR WEIGHT MAINTENANCE

	WOMEN	MEN
Calories	2,000 cal	2,500 cal
Fat	70g	95g
Saturates	20g	30g
Sugars	90g	120g
Salt	6g	6g

THE ITALIAN DIET HABIT

The Italian Diet isn't so much a strict weight-loss plan, but more a way of changing your eating habits forever. Start following the recommended plan to suit you and you'll lose weight slowly and steadily, averaging about a pound a week. It might not sound like much, but in just 14 weeks, that's equivalent to 14 pounds—and in a year, around 50 pounds! You might have lost weight more quickly in the past by following a trendy diet but the difference is, this way, you'll never feel hungry or deprived. Ultimately, you'll achieve your goal by eating really tasty food—and because you've changed your eating habits along the way, the excess weight will stay off.

To get the real benefits from *The Italian Diet*, it's also important to start living your life like an Italian! That means changing the way you think, so you are no longer "on a diet" but instead you are enjoying tasty, nutritious meals that are made from good-quality ingredients.

SHOP TILL YOU DROP

Start the pleasure cycle by filling your own shopping bags. Because of online supermarket services, it's all too easy to do all of our shopping without even looking at the products we buy until they show up on our doorstep. So get back in touch with food and enjoy shopping in your local area for the best-quality produce you can afford—food will be fresher and you'll be more likely to find local, seasonal produce, which is guaranteed to have more flavor than ingredients that have been imported from halfway across the world. Italians love to wander around local markets, selecting their fruit, vegetables, meat, fish, and bread with care. It might take a little more time to shop this way, but once you start enjoying food, you'll look at it as one of life's pleasures rather than simply another chore.

PREPARE TO BARE

For a fabulous slim body, it's important to get into the kitchen and start preparing your meals from scratch. Like shopping, once you get into the habit of cooking with fresh ingredients—rather than simply throwing a prepackaged meal into the oven—you'll find you start to take pleasure from preparing meals. Remember, 9 out of 10 Italians cook from scratch every day—and they are far less likely to have a weight problem than Americans!

COOK JUST ONE MEAL

Cooking can be stressful and time-consuming if you're preparing different meals for everyone in the family, so don't do it! Traditional Italian mammas would never dream of cooking different food for the children. Instead, everyone—young and old—eats the same dish at mealtimes.

GATHER AROUND THE DINNER TABLE

Busy lifestyles mean many of us eat on the run or while watching television. This is bad news for our waistlines, since it's much harder to monitor how much we consume when we're not paying attention to the food we are eating. In fact, many studies show a direct link between the amount of television we watch and our weight—in general, the more hours we spend watching TV, the more likely we are to be overweight or obese. In contrast, most Italian families consider every meal to be an occasion and so sit down at the table together. Meals are unrushed, with everyone enjoying good conversation and each other's company. In addition to aiding digestion, taking our time over meals helps us to recognize when we are full so that we stop eating. Our brain takes 15 minutes to register feeling full, so no matter how much food we eat during those first 15 minutes, we won't feel full.

The Italian Diet can be adapted easily if you want to eat a healthy diet without losing weight. Most women need around 2,000 calories a day to maintain their weight, while most men need around 2,500 calories. This means women who want to keep their weight steady can follow the 2,000-calorie plan (see pages 30–1). Men should also follow the 2,000-calorie plan, but can eat bigger servings of foods like bread, pasta, and rice to provide the extra calories they need and to help fill them up.

KEEP PORTIONS SMALL

We might think that traditional Italian dinners consist of huge mountains of pasta, but, in reality, most Italians eat relatively small portions. As a guide, a portion of meat, chicken, or fish should be about the size of a deck of cards. Keep an eye on portion sizes, especially when eating pasta.

ATTACK THE SNACKS

Italians rarely snack. Instead, they eat regularly and have sufficient amounts at meals to satisfy their appetite all the way through to the next meal without feeling hungry. This is good news, since many popular snack foods tend to be high in calories, which over time can pack on the pounds.

YOUR EATING PLAN

So now you're ready to get started! Fortunately, it couldn't be easier. There are two plans to choose from. One contains around 1,500 calories a day and is suitable for most women. The second contains about 2,000 calories a day and is suitable for most men. Men have bigger bodies and more muscle than women and so burn calories more quickly than women.

Along with your chosen plan, follow the guidelines below:

1. In addition to the meals, have an extra 8oz glass of skim milk every day. You can use this to make a delicious Italian cappuccino, latte, or macchiato. Milk is a really good source of calcium, which not only is important for healthy bones, but may also help to burn fat from around our waistlines.

2. Start each dinner with a bowl of salad to boost your intake of nutrients and fiber—choose a selection of ingredients from mixed greens, tomatoes, cucumber, radishes, onions, peppers, mushrooms, green beans, grated carrot, celery, arugula, watercress, and fennel. Skip the olive oil on this occasion but drizzle over some good-quality balsamic vinegar.

3. Every evening you can enjoy a drink or two. If you are following the 1,500-calorie plan, stick to 1 small glass of red or dry white wine. A glass should be no more than 125ml (roughly a sixth of a standard bottle). If you are following the 2,000-calorie plan, you can have 2 small glasses or 1 large glass (around 250ml or a third of a standard bottle) of red or dry white wine.

4. Don't add salt to your meals—all of the recipes have been devised to taste fantastic without your adding anything extra to them.

5. Use the plan to get you started on the road to weight loss. After a couple of weeks, start creating your own menu plans—each recipe is calorie-counted to help you do this.

EATING OUT ITALIAN-STYLE

It's still possible to eat out and lose weight if you follow a few simple rules:

- Dine out at traditional trattorias where meals are based on authentic recipes in small portions rather than at American-style Italian restaurants where portion sizes are usually huge.
- For a premeal nibble, choose olives and breadsticks rather than bread.
- Order an antipasti dish or *dolci* (dessert) but not both. Alternatively, choose two antipasti dishes and ask for one to be served in place of a main course.
- Steer clear of cream or cheese sauces with pasta—tomato-based sauces are better.
- Avoid tube-shaped pastas, such as rigatoni and penne, since they soak up a lot more sauce.
- Ask for half the amount of cheese on top of pizzas and ask staff to avoid brushing oil around the edge.
- Request that no oil is drizzled over dishes such as risotto, pasta, or meat.
- Skip meals described as fried, pan-fried, sautéed, or flambéed—they'll all have been cooked with a lot of oil.
- Ask for salads to come without dressing and have balsamic vinegar instead.
- Dab any excess oil off food with a napkin before starting your meal.
- Remove any visible fat from proscuitto or other meats.

THE ITALIAN DIET... IN A NUTSHELL

The Italian Diet couldn't be easier to follow, but if you'd prefer simply to enjoy some of the tasty recipes in this book without following the meal plan, check out these tips to help you eat like an Italian:

- Swap your regular cooking oil for olive oil—but still use only small amounts.
- Make your own pasta sauces rather than relying on store-bought ones to guarantee that the ingredients used are fresh. Simply fry a chopped onion in a little olive oil. When it has softened, add a can of chopped tomatoes, fresh basil, and black pepper. Simmer until the sauce has thickened, then serve with pasta.
- Don't add butter to bread—instead, mix a little olive oil with balsamic vinegar and dip your bread into this.
- Swap oil-based salad dressings for fresh lemon juice or good-quality balsamic vinegar.
- If you can't resist finishing off a bottle of wine once it's open, buy a box. That way you can stick to one small glass a night—without having the urge to finish off what's left!
- Eat five servings of fruits and veggies a day—try some you've never had before to add variety.
- Use less meat in dishes like stews, soups, and casseroles and add beans and lots of extra veggies to make it go further.
- Dispense with the salt shaker on the table and instead flavor food with garlic, fresh herbs, red wine, and black pepper.
- Eat two portions of fish a week, one of which should be an oil-rich fish.
- Swap chips, cookies, and cake for a handful of unsalted nuts or seeds when you want a snack.
- Finish meals with fresh fruit.

THE ITALIAN DIET & 1,500 CALORIE PLAN

THIS IS THE IDEAL CALORIE PLAN FOR WOMEN. FOR THE CALORIE PLAN FOR MEN PLEASE SEE PAGE 30.

The **daily calorie intake** is divided for each meal as follows:

Breakfast	250 calories
Lunch	450 calories
Dinner	600 calories
Alcohol	100 calories
Milk	100 calories
Total	1,500 calories

MONDAY

BREAKFAST
1 serving of Baked Peaches with Berries and Honey (page 37) followed by 1 slice of whole-wheat toast with 1 teaspoon each of olive oil spread and jam.

LUNCH
1 serving of Arugula and Butternut Squash Soup (page 78) followed by 1 serving of Eggplant and Cherry Tomato Hot Cups (page 65) followed by 1 peach and 1 pear.

DINNER
1 serving Grilled Shrimp with Baby Leeks and Asparagus (page 56) followed by 1 serving of Pork Steaks with Mushrooms and Rosemary (page 154) served with 4 boiled new potatoes in their skins and steamed vegetables and 1 serving of Roasted Fresh Fruits with Grand Marnier (page 170).

TUESDAY

BREAKFAST
1 serving of Fresh Fruit Skewers with Honey (page 37) with 1 individual container of low-fat plain yogurt.

LUNCH
1 serving of Three Bean and Tuna Salad with Fresh Mint (page 91) with 1 slice of ciabatta.

DINNER
1 serving of Chicken with Lemon Butter Sauce (page 150) with 2 slices of ciabatta and salad followed by 1 serving Fresh Lemon Sorbet (page 173) with mixed berries.

WEDNESDAY

BREAKFAST
1 serving of Oatmeal with Raspberries and Blueberries (page 34) and 1 small glass of freshly squeezed orange juice.

LUNCH
1 serving of Tuna and Anchovy Cakes (page 72) with salad. Plus 1 orange and 1 pear.

DINNER
1 serving of Spinach and Red Pepper Terrine (page 55) with mixed greens followed by 1 serving of Tagliatelle with Vegetables and Feta Cheese (page 100).

THE ITALIAN DIET & 1,500-CALORIE PLAN

BREAKFAST
1 sliced apple topped with
1 individual container of low-
fat plain yogurt followed by
1 Gino's Breakfast Bar
(page 42).

LUNCH
1 serving of **Light Spicy
Meatballs** (page 75)
with salad.

DINNER
1 serving of **Baked Stuffed
Onions with Sun-dried
Tomatoes** (page 53) followed
by 1 serving of **Fresh Sardines
Baked with Lemon and
Capers** (page 133) with 2 slices
of ciabatta and salad followed
by 1 apple.

THURSDAY

BREAKFAST
1 serving of **Strawberries
and Melon with Pistachio
Nuts** (page 38). Plus
1 individual container of
low-fat plain yogurt.

LUNCH
1 serving of **Pasta with
Mozzarella, Pesto, and Semi-
dried Tomatoes** (page 71).

DINNER
1 serving of **Italian Three Bean
Chili** (page 54) followed by
1 serving of **Tuna Steak with
Garlic, Olive Oil, and Chile**
(page 139) with salad.

FRIDAY

BREAKFAST
1 serving of **Grilled Tomatoes
Stuffed with Scrambled
Eggs and Smoked Salmon**
(page 39) with 1 slice of
whole-wheat toast.

LUNCH
1 serving of **Beef Carpaccio
with Mustard and Almond
Dressing** (page 97) followed
by 1 slice cantaloupe.

DINNER
1 serving of **Pizza topped
with Anchovies, Garlic, and
Black Olives** (page 115) and
salad followed by 1 bowl of
strawberries.

SATURDAY

BREAKFAST
1 serving of **Baked Eggs with
Ham in Tomato and Garlic
Sauce** (page 41) followed by
a bowl of mixed berries.

LUNCH
1 serving of **Spicy Fish Soup**
(page 81) with 2 slices of
ciabatta bread followed by
1 peach.

DINNER
1 serving of **Venison
Medallions in Red Wine** (page
163) with 4 medium-sized
boiled new potatoes.

SUNDAY

THE ITALIAN DIET & 2,000 CALORIE PLAN

THIS IS THE IDEAL CALORIE PLAN FOR MEN WHO
WANT TO LOSE WEIGHT. FOR THE CALORIE PLAN
FOR WOMEN, PLEASE SEE PAGE 28.

The **daily calorie intake** is divided
for each meal as follows:

Breakfast	400 calories
Lunch	550 calories
Dinner	750 calories
Alcohol	200 calories
Milk	100 calories
Total	2,000 calories

MONDAY

BREAKFAST
1 serving of **Oatmeal with
Raspberries and Blueberries**
(page 34) followed by 1 slice
of whole-wheat toast topped
with 1 tablespoon low-fat soft
cheese, 1 slice lean ham, and
1 tomato and 1 small glass of
freshly squeezed orange juice.

LUNCH
1 serving of **Chunky Vegetable
Soup with Barley and Pesto**
(page 82) followed by 1 serving
of **Eggplants with Tomatoes,
Garlic, and Thyme** (page 66)
followed by 1 apple.

DINNER
1 serving of **Duck Salad with
Chunky Tomato and Onion
Salad** (page 59) with 2 slices
ciabatta bread followed by
1 serving of **Linguine with
Garlic, Shrimp, and Spinach**
(page 104) followed by 1 pear.

TUESDAY

BREAKFAST
1 serving of **Strawberries
and Melon with Pistachio
Nuts** (page 38) followed by
7 tablespoons bran flakes
with skim milk.

LUNCH
1 serving of **Roasted
Tomatoes and Soft Cheese
rolled in Proscuitto** (page 68)
with salad follwed by
1 banana.

DINNER
1 serving of **Bruschetta with
Black Olive Tapenade** (page
48) followed by 1 serving of
**Fillet of Cod with a Spicy Red
Pesto** (page 132) with
½ cup cooked brown rice and
steamed vegetables.

WEDNESDAY

BREAKFAST
1 serving of **Light Banana
Shake** (page 34) followed by
1 slice of whole-wheat toast
topped with 1 teaspoon olive
oil spread, 1 poached egg,
and 2 broiled tomatoes.

LUNCH
1 serving of **Pasta with
Sun-dried Tomato Paste
and Ham** (page 71) with a
green salad followed by
1 bowl of strawberries topped
with 1 individual container of
low-fat plain yogurt and
1 teaspoon honey.

DINNER
1 serving of **Fava beans
and Fresh Mint Bruschetta**
(page 50) followed by 1
serving of **Pizza Topped with
Mozzarella, Mushrooms,
and Ham** (page 118)
with salad.

THE ITALIAN DIET & 2,OOO-CALORIE PLAN

BREAKFAST
2 **Gino's Breakfast Bars** (page 42) followed by 1 bowl fresh fruit salad and 1 small glass freshly squeezed orange juice.

LUNCH
1 serving of **Onion and Pancetta Soup** (page 84) with 3 slices of ciabatta followed by 1 bowl of mixed berries.

DINNER
1 serving of **Spicy Beef and Wild Mushroom Stew** (page 164) served with ½ cup cooked brown rice and steamed vegetables followed by 1 serving of **Grilled Vanilla Peaches with Butterscotch Sauce** (page 169).

BREAKFAST
1 serving of **Fresh Fruit Skewers with Honey** (page 37) followed by 1 individual container of low-fat plain yogurt sprinkled with 1 tablespoon chopped almonds and 2 teaspoons honey.

LUNCH
1 serving of **Egg and Salami Salad with Toasted Pine Nuts and Arugula** (page 95) and 2 slices of ciabatta followed by 1 nectarine and 1 apple.

DINNER
1 serving of **Grilled Marinated Peppers with Garlic and Proscuitto** (page 47) followed by 1 serving of **Chicken Breast with Parmesan, Tomatoes, and Mozzarella** (page 153) with salad followed by 1 apple.

BREAKFAST
1 serving of **Broiled Tomatoes Stuffed with Scrambled Eggs and Smoked Salmon** (page 39) with 2 slices whole-wheat toast topped with 2 teaspoons olive oil spread followed by 1 apple.

LUNCH
1 serving of **Sliced Tuna Steak Salad with Cherry Tomatoes, Lemon, and Garlic** (page 94) followed by 1 serving of **Chestnut and Chocolate Cake** (page 176).

DINNER
1 serving of **Lasagne** (page 183) with salad followed by 1 serving of **Hot Chocolate Cups with Pears and Amaretto** (page 175).

BREAKFAST
1 serving of **Baked Eggs with Ham in Tomato and Garlic Sauce** (page 41) with 1 slice of whole-wheat toast with 1 teaspoon olive oil spread followed by 1 pear.

LUNCH
1 serving of **Italian-style Burgers** (page 159) with salad followed by 1 orange.

DINNER
1 serving of **Bresaola and Creamed Celery Bruschetta** (page 49) followed by 1 serving of **Salmon Fillets in Tomato, Garlic, and Thyme Sauce** (page 131) with 5 boiled new potatoes in their skins and steamed vegetables

breakfast
colazione

Breakfast is the most important meal of the day, since it gets your metabolism working and kick-starts your body into action. Here I have chosen unique and versatile dishes that you will not get bored with and that will give you a great start to the day. Remember: skipping breakfast is not good for any diet—and with these tasty choices, you won't want to!

LIGHT BANANA SHAKE

Fruit shakes are not usually my kind of thing; however, the combination of the maple syrup and cinnamon with the banana is delicious. You will not feel as if you are calorie counting because it's so tasty and filling. The secret is to make sure you use ripe bananas, otherwise you won't get the smooth, sweet taste.

serves 2

189 calories	**5.5g** fat	**1g** saturates	**29g** sugars	**0.1g** salt

1 ripe banana, cut into chunks
½ teaspoon ground cinnamon
1 teaspoon maple syrup
¾ cup skim milk
2 handfuls crushed ice
2 scoops low-fat vanilla ice cream
2 teaspoons grated chocolate

1 Place the banana chunks in a blender with the cinnamon and the maple syrup. Pour in the milk and blend for 1 minute, until smooth.

2 Half-fill two serving glasses with crushed ice and pour the banana shake over the ice.

3 Add a scoop of vanilla ice cream on top and sprinkle with a little grated chocolate.

OATMEAL WITH RASPBERRIES & BLUEBERRIES

Buongiorno When I first came to England fifteen years ago, I thought that oatmeal was the most disgusting thing that you could have for breakfast. Of course, as time has gone by and I have become more British every day, I have completely changed my mind. Today, my wife often prepares oatmeal for breakfast and this is the only way I will have it! Make sure that you do add the pinch of salt, since it really does lift the flavors of the raspberries and blueberries.

serves 2

202 calories	**3.7g** fat	**0.8g** saturates	**15.3g** sugars	**0.6g** salt

½ cup rolled or steel cut oats
pinch of salt
pinch of ground cinnamon
⅓ cup raspberries (defrosted, if frozen)
⅓ cup blueberries (defrosted, if frozen)
2 tablespoons low-fat plain yogurt
1 tablespoon honey

1 Put 1½ cups water into a small saucepan and bring to a boil.

2 Slowly add the oats, stirring constantly. Lower the heat to a minimum, add the salt and the cinnamon, and let cook for 15 minutes, stirring occasionally. If you prefer a thicker consistency, cook for another 3 minutes.

3 Once the oatmeal is ready, spoon it into two serving bowls and scatter the fruits over the top.

4 Spoon the yogurt on top of the berries and drizzle the honey on top.

BAKED PEACHES WITH BERRIES & HONEY

Pesche cotte con frutti di bosco When I wrote this recipe I wasn't sure if it was for breakfast or dessert. I have chosen to put it in the breakfast chapter because I think fresh fruit gives you a lot of energy, especially in the morning, but really it will work beautifully as a dessert, too.

serves 4

128 calories **0.8g** fat **0.4g** saturates **27.7g** sugars **0.1g** salt

4 ripe but firm peaches
1 cup blueberries
¾ cup raspberries
½ cup freshly squeezed orange juice
2 tablespoons honey
¾ cup low-fat plain yogurt
1 tablespoon orange zest

1 Preheat the oven to 350°F.

2 Cut the peaches in half, remove and discard the pits, and place the fruit cut-side up in a shallow oven-proof dish.

3 Place the berries in a bowl, pour in the orange juice and honey, and mix together.

4 Fill the peach pit hollows with the berries and drizzle over the juices left in the bowl. Cook in the middle of the oven for 8 minutes.

5 Meanwhile, mix the yogurt with the orange zest. Serve two peach halves per portion, topped with a spoonful of orange-flavored yogurt.

FRESH FRUIT SKEWERS WITH HONEY

Spiedini di frutta fresca If you are feeling a little bored with the traditional breakfasts, try this dish. It's really tasty. My boys love making this and it really is a lovely and healthy way to start your day. If you are using wooden skewers, make sure they are soaked in cold water for at least 3 minutes, otherwise, they will burn under the hot broiler.

serves 4

170 calories **0.5g** fat **0.1g** saturates **41.2g** sugars **0.2g** salt

1 large banana, cut into 1in chunks
1 large red apple, peeled and cut into 1in chunks
1 melon (such as Galia), peeled, deseeded, and cut into 1in chunks
8 large strawberries
1 mango, peeled and cut into 1in chunks
2 tablespoons honey

1 Preheat the broiler to high.

2 Thread the fruit onto the skewers, alternating the types, and place on a baking sheet.

3 Drizzle the fruit skewers with the honey and place under the broiler for 5 minutes, turning them halfway through cooking. Serve warm.

HAVING FRUIT FOR BREAKFAST ALWAYS STARTS THE DAY RIGHT, AND WHY NOT START IT WITH STYLE? The crunchy pistachio nuts with the melon and strawberries give a great texture and, believe me, you will never get bored with it. I have also used this recipe as an appetizer with a couple of slices of prosciutto on top.

STRAWBERRIES & MELON WITH PISTACHIO NUTS
Melone e fragole con pistacchio

serves 2

173 calories **8.6g** fat **0.9g** saturates **19.6g** sugars **0.2g** salt

2 tablespoons pistachio nuts
2 tablespoons flaked almonds
10oz strawberries
1 Galia melon
1oz dried apricots, chopped

1 Place the pistachio nuts and almonds in a small dry frying pan and cook over medium heat for 2 minutes.

2 Toss occasionally to allow the nuts to toast evenly. Once they are ready, set them aside to cool.

3 Cut the strawberries in half and place in a large bowl.

4 Remove the seeds and the skin from the melon, cut the flesh into small bite-sized pieces, and place in the bowl with the strawberries.

5 Add the apricots and the toasted nuts and mix together. Divide between two serving bowls and enjoy.

IF YOU MAKE THIS FOR SOMEONE ELSE IT HAS TO BE THE ULTIMATE "PLEASE FORGIVE ME RECIPE." It truly is something you should find in a five-star hotel and, I promise you, it's amazing. I could have this made for me every morning, because in my opinion there is nothing better than the combination of scrambled eggs and smoked salmon. I know that this recipe may seem a little tricky, but it really is worth every second of effort. If you don't like smoked salmon, replace it with lean cooked ham.

BROILED TOMATOES STUFFED WITH SCRAMBLED EGGS & SMOKED SALMON
Pomodoro ripieno al salmone

serves 2

162 calories	**8.4g** fat	**2.2g** saturates	**3.8g** sugars	**2.2g** salt

2 large beefsteak tomatoes
2 eggs
1 egg white
2½oz sliced smoked salmon,
  cut into pieces
2 tablespoons skim milk
salt and freshly ground
  black pepper

1 Preheat the broiler to high. Cut the tomatoes in half and use a tablespoon to scoop out the flesh and seeds. Place the tomatoes under the broiler and cook for 2–3 minutes.

2 Meanwhile, place the eggs and the egg white in a bowl. Add the salmon, pour in the milk, and season with salt and pepper. Whisk together.

3 Pour the egg mixture into a medium saucepan and cook over medium heat, stirring constantly. Continue to cook, stirring, until the eggs are set to your liking.

4 Fill the warm tomatoes with the scrambled eggs, grind a little black pepper over the top, and serve immediately.

THIS IS A SIMPLE, YET DELICIOUS AND FILLING BREAKFAST RECIPE. It's perfect for the weekend and for brunch, especially if you are having friends over. And all the family will love it, too!

BAKED EGGS WITH HAM IN TOMATO & GARLIC SAUCE
Uova in camicia rossa

serves 2

223 calories   **13.9** fat   **3.2g** saturates   **6.1g** sugars   **2.3g** salt

1 tablespoon extra-virgin olive oil
1 garlic clove, sliced
1 x 14.5oz can chopped tomatoes
6 fresh basil leaves, chopped
salt and freshly ground black pepper
4 thin slices of lean ham
2 eggs

1 Preheat the oven to 350°F.

2 Heat the oil in a medium frying pan and gently fry the garlic until golden. Add in the chopped tomatoes and cook over medium heat for 10 minutes, stirring occasionally.

3 Once the sauce is ready, stir in the basil and season with salt and pepper.

4 Place the ham on the bottom of two individual baking dishes (about 4in in diameter and 2^1/$_2$in deep). Pour in the cooked tomato sauce and crack an egg over each dish. Bake in the middle of the oven for 13 minutes, or until the eggs have just set.

I HAVE TO ADMIT THAT THIS RECIPE CAME TO ME BY MISTAKE. I was trying to create something different for breakfast by mixing all kinds of ingredients from the pantry together and, if I may say so, what a masterpiece! I am so proud of my breakfast bars that I even named them after myself. If you prefer, you can substitute freshly squeezed orange juice for the apple juice. This recipe can also be used as a snack during the day.

GINO'S BREAKFAST BARS

makes 14 bars

133 calories   **4.7g** fat   **0.4g** saturates   **14.6g** sugars   **0g** salt

2oz dried mango
4oz dried figs
4oz dried apricots
½ cup almonds
½ cup sunflower seeds
⅓ cup rolled oats
½ cup whole wheat flour
¼ cup apple juice
¼ cup honey

1 Preheat the oven to 375°F.

2 Place all the dried fruits in a food processor and process until roughly chopped.

3 Fold in the almonds, sunflower seeds, oats, and flour. Pour in the apple juice with the honey and roughly process.

4 Line a baking sheet with parchment paper. Transfer the mixture onto the baking sheet and spread evenly with a knife until about $^1/_2$in thick.

5 Bake in the middle of the oven for 20 minutes, until golden brown.

6 Remove from the oven, leave on the baking sheet to cool, and slice into bars.

antipasti

Antipasti is a very important course in every Italian meal and I have chosen a great selection for you that will satisfy every palate. Some of the dishes can be used as a main course or lunch as well. Remember: if you are opting to prepare a heavy main course, try to choose a lighter appetizer that doesn't contain too many calories so it will balance your meal perfectly.

PEPERONATA IS A CLASSIC SOUTHERN ITALIAN ANTIPASTI and I have to admit this would definitely be in my top five dishes. If you have a dinner party, you can griddle the peppers in the morning and have them ready for the evening. For an alternative to prosciutto, use sliced bresaola or a lean salami of your choice. This dish also makes a great weekend lunch.

BROILED MARINATED PEPPERS WITH GARLIC & PROSCIUTTO
Peperonata con prosciutto crudo

serves 4

356 calories	**14.8g** fat	**2.9g** saturates	**11.9g** sugars	**2.7g** salt

2 red peppers
2 yellow peppers
1 green pepper
3 tablespoons extra-virgin olive oil
2 tablespoons freshly squeezed lime juice
3 garlic cloves, sliced
1 tablespoon chopped rosemary leaves
1 tablespoon salted capers, rinsed
8 slices of prosciutto, white fat removed
salt and freshly ground black pepper
8 slices of ciabatta, toasted

1 Place the peppers on a cutting board and cut in half lengthwise. Discard the seeds, membrane, and stalk and cut the flesh into $^1/_2$in strips.

2 To prepare the marinade, pour the oil in a large bowl with the lime juice, garlic, rosemary, and capers. Mix well.

3 Place the peppers in the bowl and mix together so that the marinade coats them. Cover with plastic wrap and leave at room temperature for 1 hour. Stir every 20 minutes.

4 Once they are ready, place the peppers in a colander over a large bowl to allow them to drain; reserve the marinade.

5 Heat a grill pan until very hot and cook the peppers for 15 minutes, stirring occasionally. Season with salt and pepper.

6 Meanwhile, lay 2 slices of prosciutto on each serving plate.

7 Divide the broiled pepper strips between the plates on top of the ham and drizzle over the reserved marinade. Serve each portion with 2 thin slices of toasted ciabatta.

CLASSIC ITALIAN BRUSCHETTA WITH TOMATO & BASIL

Bruschetta classica This is the ultimate bruschetta recipe—nothing beats the combination of fresh tomatoes with fresh basil on toasted ciabatta. There is only one secret to this recipe: make sure you buy the best tomatoes and let the flavors do the rest.

serves 4

280 calories	**11.3g** fat	**1.7g** saturates	**6g** sugars	**1.2g** salt

1 ciabatta loaf, cut into 8 slices, about 1in thick

18oz small plum tomatoes

10 fresh basil leaves, sliced

3 tablespoons extra-virgin olive oil

salt and freshly ground black pepper

2 garlic cloves, halved

1 Preheat a grill pan until hot and toast the ciabatta for about 3 minutes on each side, or until dark brown and crisp. Leave to cool slightly.

2 Meanwhile, quarter the tomatoes and place in a bowl. Add the basil and olive oil and season with salt and pepper. Mix everything together and cover with a kitchen towel. Set aside at room temperature for 5 minutes.

3 Lightly rub the garlic over the bread on both sides.

4 Place 2–3 tablespoons of the tomato mixture on top of each slice of bread and arrange the bruschetta on a large serving plate.

5 Drizzle with any remaining juices from the bowl of tomatoes and enjoy.

BRUSCHETTA WITH BLACK OLIVE TAPENADE

Bruschetta con crema di olive When I go back home to Naples, this is one of the dishes my mother prepares for me for our antipasti. She knows that I love olives and capers; and putting the tapenade on top of some crusty Italian bread is *buonissimo*. Make sure you use good-quality olives, or you will ruin my masterpiece! If you like, use green olives instead of black.

serves 4

289 calories	**13.7g** fat	**2g** saturates	**2.2g** sugars	**4.1g** salt

1 ciabatta loaf, cut into 8 slices, about ¾in thick

7oz pitted kalamata olives, drained

3 garlic cloves, quartered

2½ tablespoons salted capers, rinsed

2 tablespoons chopped flat-leaf parsley

2 tablespoons extra-virgin olive oil

1 tablespoon fresh lemon juice

1 Preheat a grill pan until hot and toast the ciabatta for about 3 minutes on each side, or until dark brown and crisp. Leave to cool slightly.

2 Meanwhile, place the olives, garlic, capers, and parsley in a food processor. Pour in the oil and lemon juice and start to process until you create a smooth paste. If the tapenade is too dry, add a little cold water to make it smoother.

3 Spread the tapenade over one side of the toasted ciabatta slices, arrange on a large serving plate, and enjoy.

MY WIFE, JESSIE, DIDN'T BELIEVE ME when I said that I could make celery taste sexy, so one night I went home and created this dish with her favorite cold meat, bresaola. She loved it and, I promise, so will you. The saltiness of the bresaola with the creamy sweetness of the celery is sensational—try it! If you are planning to take this dish to work for lunch, make sure the celery cream and bread are kept separate; put it together at the last minute or the bread will become soggy.

BRESAOLA & CREAMED CELERY BRUSCHETTA
Bruschetta con crema di sedano e bresaola

serves 4

191 cals **8.2g** fat **2.2g** saturates **2.7g** sugars **2.6g** salt

7oz celery (use the tender heart and the leaves)
2½oz light spreadable cheese
5 tablespoons chopped flat-leaf parsley
1 tablespoon thyme leaves
1 tablespoon Worcestershire sauce
1 tablespoon extra-virgin olive oil
salt and freshly ground black pepper
4 slices of whole wheat bread
1 garlic clove
2½oz sliced bresaola
2½oz kalamata olives, pitted and halved

1 Wash the celery and separate the very tender part with the leaves from the harder outer stalks. Cut the outer stalks on the diagonal into pieces about $^3/_4$in long and set aside.

2 Place the tender celery with the leaves in a food processor with the cheese, parsley, thyme, Worcestershire sauce, extra-virgin olive oil, and a pinch of salt and pepper. Process until smooth.

3 Meanwhile, toast the bread on both sides and then rub the garlic over one side only.

4 Use a sharp knife to cut the bresaola slices into strips.

5 Spread the celery cream over the garlicky side of the toasted bread and top with the olives.

6 Scatter the remaining celery and bresaola strips on top of the bruschetta and serve.

BRUSCHETTA IS ONE OF THE MAIN DISHES FOR AN ITALIAN ANTIPASTI. The freshness of the mint together with the fava beans is a fantastic combination that will fill you up but won't leave you feeling heavy. You can replace the fava beans with lima beans if you wish, and if you don't have fresh mint, use fresh flat-leaf parsley or chives.

FAVA BEANS & FRESH MINT BRUSCHETTA
Bruschetta con fave e menta

serves 4

337 calories **12.2g** fat **1.8g** saturates **3.3g** sugars **1.8g** salt

¾lb shelled fava beans
(fresh or frozen)
1 garlic clove
1 tablespoon freshly squeezed
lemon juice
3 tablespoons extra-virgin
olive oil
10 medium pitted green olives,
chopped
12 fresh mint leaves, finely
sliced
salt and freshly ground black
pepper
1 ciabatta loaf, cut into 8 slices
about ¾in thick

1 Half-fill a medium saucepan with water and add 1 teaspoon salt. Bring to a boil.

2 Cook the fava beans with the garlic in boiling salted water for 6 minutes, or until tender. Drain in a colander and refresh under cold water. Leave to cool.

3 Slip the beans out of their skins and place in a food processor with the garlic and lemon juice. Slowly process to a purée, adding the oil a little at the time to create a smooth, spreadable mixture. If the mixture is too thick, add a little water. Then stir in the olives and half the mint and season with salt and pepper. Set aside.

4 Preheat a grill pan until hot and toast the ciabatta for about 3 minutes on each side, or until dark brown and crisp. Leave to cool slightly.

5 Spread the bean mixture over one side of the ciabatta slices and arrange the bruschette on a large serving plate. Sprinkle on the remaining mint and serve.

I FOUND THIS RECIPE IN CASTELLAMARE, a beautiful beach town near Naples where I was working for a week, searching for new ideas and recipes. When I tried it, I immediately decided that this was going to be in my book. Make sure the sun-dried tomatoes are marinated in oil, because the dry ones are often too tough and chewy and, therefore, not good for this recipe. If you like, try red onions instead of white ones: they will work just as well.

BAKED STUFFED ONIONS WITH SUN-DRIED TOMATOES
Cipolle ripiene gratinate

serves 8

160 calories **9.2g** fat **3.9g** saturates **8.3g** sugars **0.9g** salt

4 large white onions, peeled
2 tablespoons salted capers, rinsed
10oz ricotta
½ teaspoon dried oregano
1 egg
3oz sun-dried tomatoes in oil, drained and chopped
2 tablespoons freshly grated Parmesan
4 canned anchovy fillets in oil, drained and chopped
freshly ground black pepper, to taste
drizzle of extra-virgin olive oil
salad leaves, to serve

1 Preheat the oven to 400°F.

2 Bring a medium saucepan of water to a boil, drop in the onions, and cook for 10 minutes. Drain and leave to cool slightly.

3 Cut each onion in half lengthwise from stalk to root. Scoop out and reserve the heart of the halved onions, leaving at least two outer layers to create a shell.

4 Finely chop the scooped-out onion hearts and place in a bowl. Add the capers, ricotta, oregano, egg, sun-dried tomatoes, and anchovies. Season with a little black pepper and mix together well.

5 Stuff the onion shells with the ricotta mixture and place on a greased baking sheet. Sprinkle with the Parmesan cheese and drizzle a little oil on top. Cook in the center of the oven for 30 minutes.

6 Serve 1 stuffed onion half, hot or warm, per person with your favorite salad leaves.

WHILE FILMING IN MEXICO, I SAMPLED MANY CHILI DISHES, each of them slightly different. So, of course, I felt I had to produce an Italian version of my own. This vegetable chili is packed full of delicious flavors and colors and plenty of goodness. It's very difficult to make a small amount of this chili—but you don't need to, because it can be reheated easily with no impairment to the taste.

THREE BEAN CHILI, ITALIAN-STYLE
Fagioli e peperoncino

serves 8

141 calories   **4.1g** fat   **0.6g** saturates   **10.4g** sugars   **1.2g** salt

1 small eggplant (about 10oz), cut into ¾in chunks

salt

2 tablespoons olive oil

1 onion, sliced

1 red pepper, deseeded and sliced

1 yellow pepper, deseeded and sliced

2 x 14.5oz cans chopped tomatoes

¾ cup hot vegetable stock

1 rounded tablespoon crushed, dried chile

1 x 14.5oz can cannellini beans, drained

1 x 14.5oz can cranberry beans, drained

2 zucchini, cut into ¾in cubes

7oz fine green beans, trimmed and halved

1   Place the eggplant in a colander and sprinkle generously with salt. Leave for about 20–30 minutes. Rinse and pat dry with paper towels.

2   Heat the oil in a large saucepan. Add the onion and cook over medium heat for about 5 minutes, until softened but not colored. Add the red and yellow peppers and the eggplant and cook for another 2 minutes, stirring occasionally.

3   Pour in the tomatoes and vegetable stock; add the chile and season with salt. Mix together and simmer gently for 20 minutes, uncovered, stirring occasionally.

4   Add the cannellini beans and cranberry beans along with the zucchini. Cover the pan and simmer for 5 minutes.

5   Finally, add the green beans, cover the pan again, and continue to cook for another 8 minutes. Serve hot.

SPINACH & RED PEPPER TERRINE
Sformato di vegetali

serves 6

148 calories **8.7g** fat **2.9g** saturates **4.8g** sugars **0.7g** salt

2 red peppers
1 teaspoon crushed dried chile
1 tablespoons olive oil
13oz frozen spinach
salt and freshly ground
  black pepper
9oz cottage cheese
3 eggs, lightly beaten
¼ cup freshly grated Parmesan
½ teaspoon freshly grated
  nutmeg

1 Place the peppers under a hot broiler for 20 minutes, turning halfway through, and leave until the skin turns black and blistered. Put in a bowl, cover with plastic wrap, and leave for 10 minutes. Deseed and skin the peppers and cut into strips. Place in a small bowl with the crushed dried chile and stir well.

2 Preheat the oven to 325°F. Heat the oil in a medium pan and add the frozen spinach. Cook gently over low heat for about 10 minutes, stirring continuously, until hot. Season.

3 Place the spinach in a colander and drain well. Transfer the spinach to a large bowl and stir in the cottage cheese, beaten eggs, Parmesan, and nutmeg.

4 Spread half the spinach mixture into a 2-pound nonstick loaf pan, followed by all of the red pepper and chile mixture. Carefully spread the remaining spinach over the top, trying to keep the layers separate. Cook in the center of the oven for 35 minutes, until set.

5 Leave to rest in the pan for 5 minutes, then run a sharp knife around the edges and invert onto a plate. Cut into slices and serve. This can be eaten hot or kept in the fridge and eaten cold the next day.

WHAT A GOOD-LOOKING RECIPE! THIS HAS DEFINITELY GOT THE "WOW FACTOR." If you prepare this recipe for any dinner party, your guests will be really impressed (unless, of course, they don't eat shellfish and then the evening will be ruined, but that's your fault for not asking!). Please make sure you do not overcook the shrimp, since then they become really chewy.

BROILED SHRIMP WITH BABY LEEKS & ASPARAGUS
Gamberoni e porri grigliati

serves 4

147 calories **11.8g** fat **1.7g** saturates **2.6g** sugars **0.4g** salt

7oz baby leeks

10oz asparagus stalks,
  trimmed

8 jumbo shrimp, heads and
  shells on

4 tablespoons extra-virgin
  olive oil

salt and freshly ground black
  pepper

1 lemon

1 tablespoon chopped
  flat-leaf parsley

1 Bring a medium saucepan of water to a boil and cook the leeks and asparagus for 1 minute. Drain and leave to cool slightly.

2 Place the asparagus and the leeks on a tray with the shrimp. Drizzle 2 tablespoons of the oil over the top and season with salt and pepper.

3 Heat a ridged grill pan until very hot and cook the vegetables with the shrimp for 5 minutes, turning regularly to insure an even coloring.

4 Meanwhile, pour the remaining oil into a small bowl, squeeze in the juice from half of the lemon, and add the parsley with a little salt and pepper. Whisk to combine.

5 Once the vegetables and shrimp are ready, place on a large serving dish and drizzle the dressing over the top. Cut the remaining lemon into 4 wedges and serve with the dish.

NOT OFTEN IN MY FAMILY, LIKE MOST OF YOU, DO WE EAT DUCK, UNLESS it's in between a pancake in a Chinese restaurant. However, every time I have friends over, this dish will probably be an appetizer. I make this salad, since it's very tasty; it's something most people don't make, which makes it special. It's also light and looks absolutely beautiful. Remember to dress the salad leaves at the last minute, otherwise they will become soggy from the acidity of the lime juice. It is also relatively high in fat, so try to have a low-fat main course if you are serving it to guests as an appetizer.

DUCK WITH CHUNKY TOMATO & ONION SALAD
Anatra primavera

serves 4

258 calories   **22g** fat   **5.5g** saturates   **11.5g** sugars   **0.4g** salt

2 duck breasts, skin on
4oz snow peas, shredded
7oz iceberg lettuce leaves
1 mango, diced
4 tablespoons chopped fresh mint leaves
10 flat-leaf parsley leaves
1 red onion, chopped
1 red chile, deseeded and finely chopped
3 large plum tomatoes, cut into large chunks
juice of 1 lime
salt and freshly ground black pepper

1 Preheat the oven to 400°F.

2 Use a sharp knife to score the skin of the duck in a crisscross fashion to allow the fat to drain away more easily as it cooks.

3 Place the duck, skin-side down, in an oven-proof frying pan and cook over medium heat for 4 minutes. Turn the breasts over and continue to cook for another minute. Transfer the pan to the middle of the oven and cook for 6 minutes. This timing will give you perfectly cooked pink duck breasts.

4 Remove the pan from the oven and leave the duck breasts to rest for 3 minutes.

5 Meanwhile, place the remaining ingredients in a large bowl, squeezing the lime juice over the top and seasoning with salt and pepper. Toss everything together gently and divide between four serving plates.

6 Place the duck breasts on a board and cut diagonally into slices about ¹/₄in thick.

7 Arrange the slices of duck over the salad and enjoy immediately.

lunch to go
pranzo da viaggio

Quite often you will have the dilemma of what to eat for lunch at work and will usually end up buying a sandwich or salad. Sure, you can find low-fat ones, but they can get really boring if you have to eat them every day. I have come up with some quick, tasty recipes that will make you the envy of the office—and you will know exactly what you are eating, since you have made it yourself.

I DON'T PARTICULARLY LIKE RAW ONION IN MY OMELET, so I often replace it with chives because they still give the oniony flavor. I have cooked the onions in this recipe and added chives. This is the kind of dish that my wife prepares in the morning for me to eat later for my lunch in the office or in the studio. It tastes fantastic even when it's cold.

LIGHT OMELET WITH CHIVES & POTATOES
Frittatina con erba cipollina e patate

serves 4

342 calories	**17g** fat	**3.5g** saturates	**3.3g** sugars	**0.5g** salt

3 large potatoes
3 tablespoons olive oil
salt and freshly ground black pepper
1 onion, finely sliced
5 eggs
3 tablespoons chopped chives

1 Preheat the oven to 325°F.

2 Peel the potatoes and finely slice. Lay out on a nonstick baking sheet, drizzle with 1 tablespoon of the olive oil, season, and bake for 15 minutes.

3 Select a large oven-proof frying pan about 8in diameter and 1¹/₂in deep. Heat the remaining oil in the pan, add the onions, and cook over medium heat for 5 minutes, stirring occasionally. Remove the potatoes from the oven and layer with the onions in the frying pan.

4 Lightly beat the eggs with the chives and pour over the potatoes and onions. Season with salt and freshly ground black pepper. Transfer the pan to the oven and continue to cook for 30 minutes.

5 Serve hot or at room temperature.

IF YOU WANT TO SERVE A LITTLE NIBBLE before dinner, this is the recipe to use. A friend commented that she could eat three or four of these and I wouldn't need to serve dinner, since they are so delicious, which is why this recipe it is now in my Lunch To Go section. Whatever you do, make sure you use a good-quality canned tuna, otherwise you will ruin the recipe.

BREADSTICKS WITH TUNA MOUSSE & PROSCIUTTO
Grissini con tonno e prosciutto

serves 4

278 calories **13.7g** fat **4.1g** saturates **2.1g** sugars **3.6g** salt

1 x 7oz can tuna in brine or
  spring water, drained
⅓ cup light mayonnaise
2 tablespoons chopped flat-
  leaf parsley
1 garlic clove
12 slices of prosciutto
salt and freshly ground
  black pepper
12 thick breadsticks
mixed greens, to serve

1 Place the drained tuna in a food processor with the mayonnaise, parsley, and garlic. Season with a little salt and plenty of black pepper. Process to create a smooth creamy mousse.

2 Place the slices of prosciutto on a cutting board and use a sharp knife to trim off as much fat as you can. Leave the slices spread out on the board.

3 Use a small knife to spread some of the tuna mousse on one-third of a breadstick. Place the mousse-coated part of the breadstick on a slice of prosciutto and roll up so that the ham completely encloses the mousse.

4 Repeat the process to use all the ingredients and serve the breadsticks immediately, with a little salad to accompany.

THE MOST BEAUTIFUL THING ABOUT THIS RECIPE IS that you can use it for an appetizer or a main course and, if you have any left over, you can even take it for lunch the following work day. Often, people are scared to cook eggplant because they think that it is a difficult vegetable to deal with, but this is definitely not the case. Make sure your ramekins are very deep, so that they can be packed with plenty of stuffing.

EGGPLANT & CHERRY TOMATO HOT CUPS
Coppette di melanzane

serves 6

214 calories   **10.3g** fat   **2.1g** saturates   **7.8g** sugars   **0.6g** salt

4 garlic cloves
1 tablespoon superfine sugar
1 tablespoon dried oregano
salt and freshly ground
  black pepper
3 tablespoons extra-virgin
  olive oil
12 cherry tomatoes
2 medium eggplants
¼ cup low-fat
  plain yogurt
½ teaspoon chile powder
3 eggs
1 package of filo pastry sheets
  (about 7oz)

1 Preheat the oven to 275°F.

2 Finely chop 2 of the garlic cloves and place in a small bowl with the sugar, oregano, and a pinch of salt and freshly ground black pepper. Pour in 2 tablespoons of olive oil and mix well.

3 Halve the cherry tomatoes and place cut-side up on a baking sheet. Drizzle the garlic dressing over the top and cook in the oven for about 40 minutes. Leave to cool.

4 Turn up the oven temperature to 400°F. Pierce the eggplants with a skewer and bake in the oven for about 50 minutes, until cooked and tender. Leave to cool slightly.

5 Use a tablespoon to scoop out the pulp from the eggplants (discard the skin) and place in a food processor with the remaining garlic, the yogurt, chile, and eggs. Season with salt and freshly ground black pepper and process for 10 seconds, until smooth and creamy.

6 Cut the filo pastry in 48 x 4in square shapes. Brush each sheet with the reamaining oil and overlap 4 sheets for every portion, making a total of 12 portions. Brush 12 ramekins with a little oil and line with the square filo pastry sheets.

7 Lower the oven temperature to 350°F. Fill the pastry cups with the eggplant mixture and cook in the middle of the oven for 25 minutes.

8 Remove from the oven, garnish each cup with the cooked cherry tomatoes, and serve, hot or warm, 2 cups per person.

THIS IS A GREAT VEGETARIAN DISH THAT EVEN A MEAT LOVER LIKE ME WOULD ENJOY every day of the week. Eggplants with tomatoes and garlic are the ultimate marriage made in heaven. You can replace the fresh thyme leaves with rosemary if you wish, and you can easily serve this dish to accompany absolutely anything.

EGGPLANTS WITH TOMATOES, GARLIC & THYME
Melanzane a funghetti

serves 4

296 calories **11.7g** fat **1.8g** saturates **10.3g** sugars **1.9g** salt

1 vegetable stock cube
3 medium eggplants (about 7oz each)
3 tablespoons extra-virgin olive oil
3 garlic cloves, cut in half
1 x 14.5oz can chopped tomatoes
salt and freshly ground black pepper
1 tablespoon fresh thyme leaves
3 large plum tomatoes, deseeded and cut into quarters
8 slices of bread of your choice

1 Pour 2 quarts water into a large saucepan and bring to a boil with the vegetable stock cube.

2 Prepare the eggplants by discarding the last 1/2in from both ends and any green stalk attached. Cut into 1in cubes.

3 Drop the eggplants in boiling stock and cook for 8 minutes. Drain in a colander and allow to cool. Then, slightly squeeze the eggplants in the colander to remove any excess water.

4 Heat the olive oil in a large frying pan and sizzle the garlic for 1 minute. Add the eggplants and continue to cook for 5 minutes, stirring occasionally.

5 Add in the canned tomatoes, season with salt and pepper, and continue to cook over medium heat for 15 minutes, stirring occasionally.

6 Add the thyme and the quartered fresh tomatoes and cook for another 10 minutes. Stir every couple of minutes to make sure the flavors combine well. Serve hot or cold with 2 slices of bread per portion.

PROSCIUTTO IS PROBABLY ONE OF THE MOST USED INGREDIENTS IN MY FAMILY'S MEALS and generally in my recipes, too. I absolutely love it, especially when it's combined with good tomatoes and any kind of cheese. This dish makes a great appetizer and a great lunch-box idea. Please buy good-quality tomatoes for the best flavor. If you are vegetarian, this also works fantastically with sliced broiled zucchini instead of the ham.

ROASTED TOMATOES & SOFT CHEESE ROLLED IN PROSCIUTTO
Involtini di prosciutto e pomodoro

serves 4

477 calories **18.7g** fat **5.9g** saturates **26.6g** sugars **4.3g** salt

6 large plum tomatoes
salt and freshly ground black
   pepper
2 tablespoons extra-virgin
   olive oil
7oz nonfat cream cheese
¼ cup finely chopped
   fresh chives
1½oz pitted kalamata olives,
   finely chopped
12 slices of prosciutto
¼ cup honey
8 slices of ciabatta

1 Preheat the broiler.

2 Cut the tomatoes in half and place on a baking sheet, skin-side down. Season with pepper, drizzle with the olive oil, and broil for about 10 minutes, until softened. Set aside to cool.

3 Mix the cream cheese with the chives and the olives in a medium bowl and season with salt and pepper.

4 Lay a slice of prosciutto lengthwise on a cutting board and place a tomato half on one end. Drop a teaspoon of the cream cheese mixture on top of the tomato.

5 Carefully roll up the ham to enclose the cheese and tomato. Repeat with the remaining ingredients to make 12 parcels.

6 Transfer the parcels to a serving plate, drizzle the honey on top, and serve with the sliced ciabatta.

ONE DAY, WHEN I CAME BACK FROM THE STUDIOS AFTER RECORDING *READY STEADY COOK*, I was feeling a bit hungry. I didn't want to start making a large meal and, to be honest, couldn't be bothered to start preparing something complicated. I realized that I had some leftover shrimp in the fridge. I looked in my kitchen cupboards and found a can of chick peas and some lima beans—from this came a fantastic recipe that is great for a lunch box or as an alfresco appetizer. Make sure that you eat it at room temperature and never cold from the fridge; this way, the flavors will be much better.

SHRIMP & BEAN SALAD WITH BASIL
Gamberi e fagioli all'insalata

serves 4

240 calories **8.2g** fat **1.2g** saturates **1g** sugars **4.2g** salt

1 x 14.5oz can lima beans, drained
1 x 14.5oz can chick peas, drained
10oz cooked peeled shrimp
1 garlic clove, crushed
2 tablespoons extra-virgin olive oil
juice of 2 limes
10 basil leaves
salt and freshly ground black pepper

1 Put the beans, chick peas, shrimp, and garlic in a large bowl. Pour over the oil and the lime juice.

2 Tear the basil leaves into pieces, add to the bowl, and season with salt and pepper.

3 Gently mix everything together, cover with plastic wrap, and leave to rest in the fridge overnight. (If you can, mix the salad at least twice to allow the flavors to combine.)

4 Before serving, bring the salad to room temperature, so you can enjoy the flavors better.

FOR ANY ITALIAN, THE ULTIMATE LUNCH-BOX DISH HAS TO BE A GOOD PASTA SALAD. There are millions of variations, but I like mozzarella, pesto, and tomatoes for a perfect combination. Make sure the pasta is cooked al dente, otherwise it may get soggy.

THE ULTIMATE PASTA SALAD

serves 2

457 calories   **19.5g** fat   **9.9g** saturates   **4.6g** sugars   **1.6g** salt

salt and freshly ground
   black pepper
5oz dried bow-tie pasta
1 tablespoon good-quality
   pesto Genovese (pesto
   made with basil and
   pine nuts)
5oz baby mozzarella balls
2 tablespoons semi-dried
   tomatoes in oil, drained

1 Pour 1¹/₂ quarts of water into a large saucepan with a pinch of salt and bring to a boil. Cook the pasta in boiling salted water until al dente (that is, 1 minute less than instructed on the package).

2 Drain the pasta in a colander and rinse immediately under cold water to prevent it from cooking further. Set aside for 5 minutes, and shake it well every minute to make sure that all the water drains off.

3 Meanwhile, place the rest of the ingredients in a large bowl, seasoning to taste.

4 Add the pasta into the bowl and gently mix everything together. Let rest at room temperature for 10 minutes, stirring occasionally so that the flavors combine well. Then, serve immediately, or keep in a sealed container in the fridge for the following day. Do not keep longer than 48 hours.

I LEARNED HOW TO MAKE RED PESTO WHEN I WAS VACATIONING ON THE LIGURIAN COAST in a place called San Remo, where basil pesto is a very big part of their culture. Of course, to make red pesto you have to substitute the fresh basil with sun-dried tomatoes and, believe me, once you have tried this, it will become a regular lunch to go for you—tasty and filling, yet still very fresh. You can also use the red pesto for a dip or even spread it on broiled chicken or fish. For the best flavor, make sure the sun-dried tomatoes are marinated in oil and not completely dry, and never use fresh pasta for this dish.

PASTA WITH SUN-DRIED TOMATO PASTE & HAM
Fusilli al pesto rosso

serves 4

399 calories	**7.8g** fat	**1.1g** saturates	**8.3g** sugars	**2.6g** salt

**salt and freshly ground
black pepper**
10oz dried fusilli
6 basil leaves
**5oz sun-dried tomatoes in oil
(reserve the oil)**
**5oz lean cooked ham, cut into
1in strips**
**½ cup canned corn,
drained**

1 Pour 4 quarts water into a large saucepan with a pinch of salt and bring to a boil. Cook the pasta in boiling salted water until al dente (that is, 1 minute less than instructed on the package).

2 Drain the pasta in a colander and rinse immediately under cold water to prevent it from cooking more. Once cold, set aside for 5 minutes, shaking it well every minute to make sure that all the water drains off.

3 Meanwhile, place the basil and the sun-dried tomatoes with their oil in a food processor. Process to create a smooth paste. If the paste is too dry, add a little cold water to loosen it. Transfer the sun-dried tomato paste into a large bowl.

4 Add the ham, corn, and pasta to the bowl and gently mix everything together. Cover with plastic wrap and let stand at room temperature for 15 minutes, stirring every 5 minutes so that the flavors combine well.

5 Serve immediately, or keep in a sealed container in the fridge for the following day. Do not keep longer than 48 hours.

IN MY KITCHEN CUPBOARDS YOU WILL ALWAYS FIND CANNED TOMATOES, canned beans, and canned tuna; mainly because I really believe that they are base ingredients for many recipes. My tuna and anchovy cakes are one of my favorite dishes to prepare for a family meal or for dinner parties, because they are very easy to create and yet extremely tasty. A fantastic dish to use hot as a main course, or for lunch the day after.

TUNA AND ANCHOVY CAKES
Timballo di tonno e acciughe

serves 4

332 calories **3.9g** fat **0.8g** saturates **1.9g** sugars **2.4g** salt

9oz russet potatoes, peeled and quartered
salt and freshly ground black pepper
2 slices of white bread, crusts removed, soaked in water and squeezed
8 canned anchovy fillets in oil, drained and finely chopped
1 egg
grated zest of 1 lemon
2 x 7oz cans tuna chunks in water, drained
1 garlic clove, finely chopped
¼ cup chopped flat-leaf parsley
1½ cups good-quality fine bread crumbs, toasted

1 Boil the potatoes in a large pan of salted water until soft. Drain, mash, and pour into a large bowl. Let cool.

2 Add the bread, anchovies, egg, lemon zest, tuna, garlic, parsley, salt, and pepper. Mix everything together until evenly combined.

3 Preheat the oven to 350°F.

4 Use your hands to form the mixture into four balls, each more or less the size of a tennis ball. Gently flatten, then coat the cakes in the toasted bread crumbs.

5 Place the tuna cakes on a baking sheet lined with parchment paper and bake in the oven for 20 minutes, or until golden brown.

6 Serve hot, or at room temperature, with mixed greens and lemon wedges.

I BELIEVE THAT GETTING CHILDREN INVOLVED IN COOKING IS A GREAT IDEA and this is one recipe that makes it easy to do that. Every time I make meatballs at home my boys love to get involved, and, of course, because they've made them, they feel very proud when they eat them. You don't have to use chile flakes, and you can definitely substitute the ground beef with pork or lamb, if you prefer.

LIGHT SPICY MEATBALLS
Polpette di carne piccanti

serves 6

439 calories **17.8g** fat **6g** saturates **12.1g** sugars **1.9g** salt

1lb lean ground beef
4 garlic cloves, crushed
3 cups fresh, cubed white bread crumbs
¼ cup chopped flat-leaf parsley
½ cup freshly grated Parmesan
1 teaspoon dried chile flakes
½ teaspoon paprika
salt and freshly ground black pepper
1 egg
3 x 8oz cans tomato sauce
10 basil leaves
3 tablespoons olive oil
10oz cooked brown rice

1 Put the ground beef, garlic, bread crumbs, parsley, Parmesan, chile flakes, and paprika in a large bowl. Season with salt and break in the egg. Mix all the ingredients thoroughly with your hands, then shape into 12 equal-sized balls. Place on a plate, cover with plastic wrap, and let rest in the fridge for 20 minutes.

2 Meanwhile, pour the tomato sauce into a large saucepan and place over medium heat. Season with salt and pepper, add the basil leaves, bring to a boil, then remove from the heat.

3 Heat the olive oil in a large nonstick frying pan and gently fry the meatballs over medium heat for 5 minutes, until golden brown all over.

4 Place the meatballs in the tomato sauce and return the pan to low heat. Cook for 1 hour with the lid half on, stirring occasionally. If the sauce becomes too thick, add a little water.

5 To serve, divide the rice between six serving plates, place 2 meatballs on each serving, and spoon over the tomato sauce.

6 Serve hot or at room temperature.

soups & salads

zuppe e insalate

Soups and salads are perfect for lunch or a light supper, often containing low amounts of calories and fat, but large amounts of flavor. I love soups, since they are so useful for using up leftovers, and these salads are so satisfying, especially if you use the best-quality ingredients you can find.

MY WIFE OFTEN MAKES THIS SOUP AND WE LOVE IT. She used to cook it in butter and add cream, but I proved to her that my recipe has the same taste with far fewer calories and fat. These days, she will only cook it Gino's way! You can substitute the butternut squash with pumpkin and, if you make a big batch, it can be kept refrigerated for at least 48 hours. An excellent soup to take to the office, too.

ARUGULA & BUTTERNUT SQUASH SOUP
Zuppa di zucca e rucola

serves 6

117 cals   **4.5g** fat   **0.6g** saturates   **5.5g** sugars   **1.4g** salt

2 tablespoons extra-virgin
  olive oil
1 onion, roughly chopped
1 medium butternut squash
1 large potato, peeled and cut
  into quarters
5 cups vegetable stock
salt and freshly ground
  black pepper
5oz arugula leaves

1 Heat the oil in a large saucepan over medium heat and fry the onion for 2 minutes, stirring occasionally.

2 Meanwhile, use a sharp knife to peel the butternut squash and scoop out the seeds. Cut the flesh into chunks. Add the squash and the potatoes to the saucepan and continue to fry for another 2 minutes.

3 Pour in the stock, bring to a boil, and cook over low heat for 40 minutes, uncovered, stirring every 10 minutes.

4 Use a hand blender to process into a smooth, creamy soup. Season with salt and pepper.

5 Serve hot, garnished with the arugula leaves.

EVERY TIME I MAKE THIS SOUP, I CAN'T BELIEVE HOW EASY IT IS and, yet, it is so tasty and good for you. I strongly believe that we should all eat more fish, because it's a great source of protein and contains lots of vitamins. If you have any soup left over, it can be refrigerated for 24 hours, but please remember that it can be reheated only once.

SPICY FISH SOUP
Zuppa di pesce piccante

serves 6

262 calories **9.2g** fat **0.9g** saturates **6.6g** sugars **1.1g** salt

24 uncooked jumbo shrimp, shells on

2 cups fish stock

3 tablespoons extra-virgin olive oil

1 large onion, finely chopped

1 teaspoon dried chile flakes

7oz roasted red peppers in brine from a jar, drained and sliced

¾ cup white wine

1 x 14.5oz can chopped tomatoes

salt

14oz haddock, skinned and cut into 2in chunks

14oz red mullet, skinned and cut into 2in chunks

¼ cup chopped flat-leaf parsley

1 Shell the shrimp, but leave the tails on. Add the shells to the fish stock and simmer for 5–10 minutes, since they add so much flavor. Set aside.

2 Heat the oil in a large saucepan over medium heat and fry the onion, chile, and red peppers for 5 minutes, stirring occasionally.

3 Pour in the wine and continue to cook for another 3 minutes to evaporate the alcohol.

4 Pour in the fish stock, add the chopped tomatoes and season with salt. Bring to a boil, lower the heat to medium and cook, uncovered, for 20 minutes.

5 Add the fish and the shrimp, stir everything together, and continue to cook for 6 minutes.

6 Add the parsley, check the seasoning, and serve immediately.

A GOOD MINESTRONE SHOULD ALWAYS BE MADE WITH FRESH VEGETABLES, so don't even think about using frozen vegetables for this dish. For the Italians, this soup is like chicken soup is for Americans: it will cure any symptoms of early illness that may occur (obviously, please see a doctor if you are really ill!). If you prefer, you can substitute the pearl barley with any long-grain rice available.

CHUNKY VEGETABLE SOUP WITH BARLEY & PESTO
Minestrone

serves 4

205 calories **4.5g** fat **0.6g** saturates **6.5g** sugars **2.2g** salt

½ cup pearl barley, soaked in cold water for 3 hours, drained

1 onion, cut into ½in cubes

1 carrot, cut into ½in cubes

2 celery sticks, cut into ½in cubes

4oz green cabbage, roughly sliced

1 russet potato, peeled and cut into ½in cubes

1 quart vegetable stock

1 zucchini, cut into ½in cubes

salt and freshly ground black pepper

15 basil leaves

2 garlic cloves

drizzle of extra-virgin olive oil

1 Place the barley in a saucepan, cover with cold water, and bring to a boil. Cook for 25 minutes, until tender. Drain and set aside.

2 Meanwhile, place the prepared onion, carrot, celery, cabbage, and potato in a large saucepan. Pour in the stock and bring to a boil.

3 Once it starts to boil, add the zucchini, lower the heat, and simmer for 15 minutes. Season with salt and pepper and stir occasionally.

4 Meanwhile, place the basil in a food processor with the garlic and pour in 8 tablespoons of the hot stock. Process to create a smooth, runny paste.

5 Pour the pesto into the pan containing the vegetables and add the barley. Stir until everything is well combined and check the seasoning.

6 Serve immediately, garnished with a little drizzle of extra-virgin olive oil on top.

YOU MIGHT LOOK AT THE TITLE OF THIS RECIPE AND NOT WANT TO TRY IT, since the combination seems a little odd, but please trust me, because the flavors work just perfectly together— it's a beautiful soup to have for an appetizer. You can substitute the cannellini beans with cranberry beans, if you wish.

CANNELLINI BEAN & SHRIMP SOUP
Zuppa di fagioli e gamberi

serves 6

153 cals	**5g** fat	**0.6g** saturates	**6.4g** sugars	**3.4g** salt

1 x 15.5oz can cannellini beans, drained

1½ quarts vegetable stock

2 tablespoons extra-virgin olive oil

6 celery sticks, roughly chopped

2 onions, roughly chopped

1 x 14.5 can chopped tomatoes

freshly ground black pepper

1 teaspoon chopped thyme leaves

9oz cooked, peeled shrimp

1 Place half the beans in a food processor with $^3/_4$ cup vegetable stock and process until smooth.

2 Heat the oil in a large saucepan and add the celery and onions. Cook over medium heat for 5 minutes, stirring occasionally, until the vegetables begin to brown.

3 Add the tomatoes and continue to cook for another 5 minutes.

4 Pour in the remaining stock with the whole beans and the bean purée. Season with pepper, add the thyme, and bring to a boil.

5 Reduce the heat, cover the pan, and simmer for 35 minutes, stirring occasionally.

6 Add the shrimp and continue to cook for another 5 minutes. Serve immediately.

BY FAR, AND I REALLY MEAN BY FAR, this has to be my favorite soup recipe in this book. Actually, I'm confidently stating that it is my favorite soup in my last three books! Once you have tried it, you will be amazed by the flavors and the combination of ingredients.

ONION & PANCETTA SOUP
Brodo di cipolla e pancetta

serves 4

288 calories **18.7g** fat **6.5g** saturates **12.8g** sugars **3.4g** salt

4oz pancetta or bacon,
   rinds removed,
   cut into ½in pieces
2 tablespoons extra-virgin
   olive oil
1½lb white onions, finely
   sliced
5 cups chicken stock
1 x 14.5oz can chopped tomatoes
salt and freshly ground
   black pepper
6 fresh basil leaves, shredded
¼ cup freshly grated
   Parmesan

1 Place a large saucepan over medium heat and start to sizzle the pancetta or bacon for 2 minutes, stirring constantly.

2 Pour in the oil with the onions and stir everything together. Lower the heat and cook for 20 minutes, stirring occasionally, until the onions are a beautiful golden color.

3 Once the onions are colored, pour in the chicken stock and the chopped tomatoes. Season with salt and pepper and bring to a boil. Lower the heat, half-cover the pan with the lid and simmer for 30 minutes, stirring occasionally. Five minutes before the end of this time, check the consistency of the soup and add a little more stock if it is too thick.

4 Just before serving, stir in the basil and check the seasoning. Serve hot with a sprinkle of Parmesan on top.

IF YOU LOVE CARROTS AND YOU ARE FED UP WITH THE USUAL WAY OF COOKING THEM, this recipe will really rock your world. In my house, we only eat carrots this way and every time my wife prepares them, there are never any left over. A great dish to accompany any kind of fish or meat or even mixed with your favorite salad, it's perfect for a packed lunch, since it can be prepared 24 hours in advance. If you are making a big batch, it will keep refrigerated easily for 3 days, but whatever you do, make sure you eat it at room temperature.

MARINATED CARROTS WITH FRESH MINT & ALMONDS
Carote alla scapece

serves 2

274 calories   **20g** fat   **2.5g** saturates   **17.4g** sugars   **0.6g** salt

3 large carrots
salt
10 mint leaves, finely sliced
pinch of dried chile flakes
¼ cup slivered almonds
2 tablespoons extra-virgin olive oil
3 tablespoons white wine vinegar

1 Peel the carrots and cut into $^1/_2$in rounds.

2 Half-fill a medium saucepan with water, add a pinch of salt, and bring to a boil. Drop in the carrots and cook for 2 minutes, drain, and place in a large bowl.

3 While the carrots are still hot, add the rest of the ingredients to the bowl. Season with a little salt and gently mix everything together.

4 Set aside at room temperature for 20 minutes to allow the flavors to combine. Gently stir every 5 minutes. Serve as a side dish or mixed with a salad of your choice.

IF YOU NEED A QUICK SALAD THAT WILL TAKE YOU LESS THAN 4 MINUTES TO MAKE from start to finish, then this is the one you should try. It is fresh, light, colorful, and, of course, really, really tasty. It's great for an appetizer or to accompany any fish or meat. Substitute the cannellini beans with chick peas, if you like, and make sure you use good-quality Italian extra-virgin olive oil.

ZUCCHINI RIBBONS WITH CANNELLINI BEANS & LEMON DRESSING
Zucchine, limone e fagioli

serves 4

128 cals	**6.3g** fat	**0.9g** saturates	**4g** sugars	**0.8g** salt

4 zucchini

1 lemon

1 x 15.5oz can cannellini beans, drained

2 tablespoons chopped chives

1 tablespoon chopped flat-leaf parsley

salt and freshly ground black pepper

2 tablespoons extra-virgin olive oil

1 Slice the zucchini thinly lengthwise using a swivel-bladed peeler. (Try not to use too much of the center of the zucchini, since it is less tasty.) Bring a medium saucepan of water to a boil and cook the strips for 1 minute. Drain and place in a large bowl.

2 Grate the zest of half the lemon over the top and squeeze in the juice of the whole lemon. Add the cannellini beans with the chives and parsley, and season with salt and pepper. Pour in the oil and mix well. Leave to marinate for 2 minutes before serving.

3 Serve at room temperature.

THIS SIMPLE LITTLE SALAD IS FULL OF GREAT TEXTURES AND FLAVORS to awaken those taste buds. What's more, I had to make a salad that would remind me of my home country, hence, the beautiful colors of the Italian flag. If you can't find watermelon in the supermarket you could use a sweet, orange-fleshed cantaloupe melon. Then the dish will remind you of Ireland!

FETA, WATERMELON & BASIL SALAD
Feta e anguria

serves 4

273 calories **21.4g** fat **9.9g** saturates **8.4g** sugars **2.7g** salt

7oz fine green beans, trimmed and halved

12oz watermelon flesh

9oz feta, cubed

1oz fresh basil leaves, shredded

2 pinches of garlic salt

3 tablespoons extra-virgin olive oil

1 tablespoon balsamic vinegar

1 tablespoon lemon juice

a little freshly ground black pepper

1 Bring a pan of water to a boil and cook the green beans for 3–4 minutes. Drain and plunge into cold water to cool.

2 Cut the watermelon into bite-sized chunks and place in a serving bowl, together with the feta and the drained and cooled green beans. Scatter the basil over the top.

3 Put all the remaining ingredients into a small pot or jar with a lid. Shake well, and drizzle the dressing over the salad.

4 Mix well and serve.

MOZZARELLA ALWAYS SEEMS TO BE PAIRED UP WITH TOMATO, BASIL, OR AVOCADO in the US, and, although these are fantastic combinations, there are so many other ways of eating it. The partnership of the crunchy French beans, garlic, and pine nuts is just perfect for any palate. Remember that you should always use buffalo mozzarella in salads or on its own. Never cook with it, because when it's heated, it will release too much milk and make your dish very watery. When cooking, use a standard cow's mozzarella.

WARM FRENCH BEAN SALAD WITH MOZZARELLA & GARLIC
Fagiolini e mozzarella

serves 2

281 calories **23.7g** fat **9.8g** saturates **2.1g** sugars **1.1g** salt

1 tablespoon pine nuts
salt and freshly ground
  black pepper
6oz French beans, trimmed
½ garlic clove
8 basil leaves
1 tablespoon extra-virgin
  olive oil
1 tablespoon lemon juice
1 buffalo mozzarella ball (5oz),
  drained and cut into 8 pieces

1 Put the pine nuts in a small dry frying pan and place over medium heat for 4 minutes, tossing occasionally so that the nuts toast evenly. Allow to cool and set aside.

2 Bring a medium saucepan of salted water to a boil and cook the beans for 3 minutes, or until al dente.

3 Meanwhile, finely chop the garlic and the basil together and place in a large bowl. Pour in the oil and lemon juice and mix until well combined.

4 Drain the beans and, while they are still hot, place into the bowl with the dressing.

5 Season with salt and pepper and toss everything together until evenly coated. Divide between two serving plates.

6 Top with the mozzarella cheese and the pine nuts.

7 Enjoy while the beans are still warm.

TONNO E FAGIOLI HAS TO BE ONE OF THE MOST WELL-KNOWN SALADS IN ITALY. The reason for this is very simple: the flavors work together beautifully. The sweetness of the red onion partnered with the freshness of the mint and the beans are truly a combination made in heaven. This dish can be prepared a couple of hours before serving and is a great one to take to the office the next day—if there is any left over. If you prefer, you can serve this salad with plain crackers instead of the garlic bread.

THREE BEAN & TUNA SALAD WITH FRESH MINT
Insalata tonno e fagioli

serves 6

372 calories   **8g** fat   **1.2g** saturates   **5.3g** sugars   **2.4g** salt

1 x 15.5oz can chick peas, drained

1 x 15.5 can red kidney beans, drained

1 x 15.5oz can lima beans, drained

1 red onion, finely sliced

1 lemon

2 tablespoons extra-virgin olive oil

2 tablespoons chopped mint leaves

salt and freshly ground black pepper

12 thin slices of ciabatta

1 garlic clove

2 x 7oz cans tuna in brine or spring water, drained

1 Place all the beans in a large bowl with the sliced onion. Squeeze in the juice of half the lemon and pour in the oil. Add the mint and season with salt and pepper. Mix everything together and leave to rest for 10 minutes at room temperature.

2 Meanwhile, toast the ciabatta on both sides and rub the garlic on the toasted bread slices. Place each slice in the center of a serving plate.

3 Gently fold the tuna into the bean salad and serve on top of the garlic bread.

THIS IS A WONDERFULLY COLORFUL SALAD that is bursting with flavor and goodness from the seafood and an array of vegetables. It's also great for al fresco dining, whether you are entertaining or not!

SEAFOOD SALAD WITH CAPERS & LEMON
Insalata di mare con capperi e limoni

serves 4

274 calories **11.2g** fat **1.9g** saturates **8.3g** sugars **1.4g** salt

1 large carrot
1 red pepper
1 yellow pepper
1 large zucchini
salt and freshly ground
  black pepper
12oz uncooked shrimp, peeled
12oz medium squid,
  cleaned and cut into rings
  ¼in thick
3 tablespoons extra-virgin
  olive oil
2 lemons
2 tablespoons small capers in
  vinegar, drained
7oz arugula leaves
balsamic vinegar

1 Trim the carrot, peppers, and zucchini and cut into strips about 2¹/₂in long and ¹/₄in thick.

2 Fill a large saucepan three-quarters full with water and add a pinch of salt. Bring to a boil and cook the shrimp, squid, and vegetables for 2 minutes. Drain and place in a bowl. Leave until just warm.

3 Meanwhile, prepare the dressing by pouring the oil into a small bowl with 1 tablespoon freshly squeezed lemon juice, salt, and pepper. Whisk together until well combined.

4 Pour the dressing over the seafood and vegetables, add the capers, and mix well. Leave to marinate for 1 minute.

5 Divide the arugula leaves between four individual plates or one large serving plate and drizzle a little balsamic vinegar over the top. Place the seafood salad on top of the arugula leaves and serve immediately.

GREMOLATA IS NOTHING MORE THAN PARSLEY, GARLIC, AND LEMON ZEST CHOPPED TOGETHER. Originally, it was created in Italy to give an extra twist to any fish or meat dish. I think it is a fantastic idea, especially with tuna, because I often feel that when you eat fish, you need something fresh to cleanse your palate. Try this recipe with swordfish, too—it will work just as well.

SLICED TUNA STEAK SALAD WITH CHERRY TOMATOES, LEMON & GARLIC
Tagliata di tonno con gremolata

serves 2

374 calories **23.8g** fat **4.3g** saturates **1.3g** sugars **0.7g** salt

2 tablespoons flat-leaf parsley

1 garlic clove

1 lemon

2 tuna steaks, about 6oz each and about ¼ to ½in thick

3 tablespoons extra-virgin olive oil

salt and freshly ground black pepper

3oz arugula leaves

5 cherry tomatoes, halved

1 tablespoon good-quality balsamic vinegar

1 Preheat a griddle pan until very hot.

2 To prepare the gremolata, place the parsley and the garlic on a cutting board and finely chop with a sharp knife. Place in a bowl and grate the zest of half the lemon over the top. Mix and set aside.

3 Rub the tuna steaks with 2 tablespoons of the oil. Cook on the griddle pan for 1 minute on each side. Then season with salt and pepper and place on a cutting board to rest for 1 minute.

4 Meanwhile, place the arugula leaves and the tomatoes in a large bowl, pour over the remaining oil and the balsamic vinegar. Season with salt and pepper and mix well using your fingertips. Arrange the arugula leaves and tomatoes on two serving plates.

5 Cut the tuna into ¹/₂in slices using a sharp knife and lay on top of the arugula. Drizzle over the gremolata and serve.

THIS RECIPE IS DEDICATED TO MY ELDEST SON, LUCIANO. He could eat eggs, salami, and nuts every day if I'd let him, so I tried to create a dish that would have all those ingredients in it and... here it is, and I must admit that it is delicious. If you like, you can substitute the salami with lean cooked ham or use quail eggs instead of normal eggs. I have also tried this dish with walnuts instead of pine nuts and it's absolutely *fantastico*.

EGG & SALAMI SALAD WITH TOASTED PINE NUTS & ARUGULA

Insalata di uova e pinoli

serves 4

288 calories **23.2g** fat **5g** saturates **6.7g** sugars **0.9g** salt

4 eggs
2½ tablespoons pine nuts
4oz arugula leaves
10oz mixed greens
1 yellow pepper, deseeded and thinly sliced
8 slices of Salame Napoli, cut into strips
salt and freshly ground black pepper
3 tablespoons extra-virgin olive oil
1 tablespoon balsamic vinegar
4 large plum tomatoes, quartered

1 Cook the eggs in a small pan of boiling water for 7 minutes. Leave under cold running water for 1 minute and shell. Cut into quarters lengthwise.

2 Meanwhile, put the pine nuts in a small dry frying pan and place over medium heat for 2 minutes, tossing occasionally, until just colored. Set aside to cool.

3 Place the mixed greens in a large bowl and add the pine nuts, yellow pepper, and salami. Season with salt and black pepper, then pour in the extra-virgin olive oil and the balsamic vinegar. Gently mix everything together and divide between four individual plates or one large serving plate. Arrange the eggs and tomatoes on top of the salad and serve.

FOR THOSE OF YOU WHO LOVE TO CREATE STYLISH DISHES FOR FANCY PARTIES, this will definitely be an appetizer to choose. In Italy, we eat a lot of carpaccio, simply because it's extremely tasty and light, so I thought that this recipe had to be in this book. Make sure you get a good-quality beef tenderloin, because it will make a huge difference to the final result.

BEEF CARPACCIO WITH MUSTARD & ALMOND DRESSING
Insalata con carpaccio

serves 2

411 calories   **33.1g** fat   **6.5g** saturates   **2.2g** sugars   **1.3g** salt

5oz lean beef tenderloin, cut into four pieces
juice of 1 lemon
2 tablespoons extra-virgin olive oil
2 tablespoons light mayonnaise
1 teaspoon Dijon mustard
2 eggs
3oz arugula leaves
3oz frisée lettuce
¼ cup slivered almonds, toasted
salt and freshly ground black pepper

1 Place the four raw steak pieces between two sheets of plastic wrap on a cutting board. Use a meat mallet to beat the steaks until very thin (or you can use the base of a heavy pan to do the job). Remove the plastic wrap and lay the meat on two individual dishes or one big serving dish.

2 Squeeze the lemon juice into a bowl and pour in the oil. Whisk well with a fork.

3 Brush the lemon dressing all over the meat, ensuring that every part has been covered. Reserve the leftover dressing. Cover the plates with plastic wrap and leave to rest in the fridge for 50 minutes.

4 Meanwhile, place the mayonnaise in a bowl with the mustard. Pour in 1 tablespoon water, which makes the dressing easier to drizzle over the meat.

5 Cook the eggs in boiling water for no more than 6 minutes, so the yolks don't overcook. Cool them under cold running water for 1 minute.

6 Just before serving, place the salad leaves in a bowl and dress with the remaining lemon dressing.

7 Once everything is ready, remove the plastic wrap from the plates, drizzle the mustard dressing over the beef carpaccio, and place the salad in the center.

8 Shell and halve the eggs and place near the salad. Finally, sprinkle with the slivered almonds, season, and serve immediately.

pasta, pizza e risotto

Many of you believe that carbs are a really big no-no in the diet world. But considering that Italians have eaten this kind of food at least once a day for generations and still maintain a good physique and healthy lifestyle, I think it proves that it's all about portion control and not adding in lots of other ingredients that are loaded with fat. Remember, Italians are the least likely people in Europe to be obese!

WHILE I WAS ON VACATION IN TURKEY, I ATE A LOT OF SALADS with feta cheese, and so when I came home I tried it with pasta. Let me tell you what a fantastic combination it is. The feta cheese gives the tagliatelle a great creamy texture and yet remains colorful and light. Do not overcook the tagliatelle, otherwise the dish will be sticky and soggy.

TAGLIATELLE WITH VEGETABLES & FETA
Tagliatelle con verdure

serves 4

408 calories **16.1g** fat **4g** saturates **10.4g** sugars **0.8g** salt

¼ cup extra-virgin olive oil

1 red onion, finely sliced

1 eggplant, cut into ½in cubes

1 yellow pepper, deseeded and cut into ½in cubes

2 zucchini, cut into ½in cubes

4oz cherry tomatoes, halved

salt and freshly ground black pepper

9oz fresh or dried egg tagliatelle

10 basil leaves

2½oz feta cheese, cubed

1 Heat the oil in a large frying pan and fry the onion for 2 minutes, until softened but not colored.

2 Add the eggplant and cook for 5 minutes, then add the yellow pepper and continue to cook for 3 minutes, stirring occasionally.

3 Add the zucchini and the tomatoes and season with salt and black pepper. Continue to cook for another 8 minutes, stirring occasionally.

4 Meanwhile, cook the pasta in a large saucepan in plenty of boiling salted water, until al dente. Drain and transfer to the frying pan with the vegetables. Stir together over low heat for 30 seconds to allow the flavors to coat the pasta. Remove from the heat, mix in the basil and cheese, and serve.

IF YOU HAVE EVER LOOKED FOR A TRADITIONAL NEAPOLITAN RECIPE, you have just found it! *Pasta e fagioli* is to the Neapolitans like Guinness is to the Irish. This will be enjoyed in any Neapolitan household at least twice a week. There are many variations of it: some people make it with mussels, others with shrimp, but my personal favorite has to be with porcini mushrooms. If you can buy them in season, substitute the dried porcini mushrooms with 6oz fresh porcini. This is a fantastic pasta dish that can be reheated the day after and will still retain the same wonderful flavors.

SPICY PASTA WITH PORCINI MUSHROOMS & CANNELLINI BEANS
Pasta e fagioli piccante con funghi porcini

serves 4

432 calories   **8g** fat   **1.2g** saturates   **5.7g** sugars   **1.2g** salt

1oz dried porcini mushrooms
1 leek
2 tablespoons olive oil
⅓ cup white wine
⅓ cup vegetable stock
4oz frozen peas, defrosted
½ teaspoon dried chile flakes
1 x 15.5oz can cannellini beans, drained
salt
2 tablespoons chopped rosemary leaves
10oz dried pasta shells

1 Place the mushrooms in a bowl and soak in warm water for 20 minutes. Once they are soft, squeeze to remove excess water, and set aside. Reserve ⅓ cup of the soaking water.

2 Wash the leek and discard the green part. Cut the white part into thin rings.

3 Heat the oil in a large saucepan and fry the leek over medium heat for 5 minutes, stirring occasionally.

4 Add the mushrooms and the wine and continue to cook for 1 minute. Pour in the reserved mushroom-soaking water and the stock, along with the peas, the chile, and the beans. Season with salt, add the rosemary, and stir. Let cook for another 6 minutes over medium heat, stirring occasionally.

5 Meanwhile, cook the pasta in a large saucepan in plenty of boiling salted water, until al dente. Drain well and transfer to the saucepan with the sauce. Stir everything together over low heat for 1 minute, then serve immediately.

I HAVE TO ADMIT THAT MY MOTHER IS NOT THE BEST COOK IN THE WORLD unless cooking the traditional Neapolitan dishes she has grown up with. However, this has to be one of her best creations, which she prepares for me every time I go to visit her. It is very important for this recipe to use canned cherry tomatoes, because if you use the fresh ones, the sauce will be too watery. Do not overcook the shrimp or langoustines, otherwise they will get tough and chewy.

MIXED SEAFOOD LINGUINE WITH CHILE & CHERRY TOMATOES
Linguine ai frutti di mare

serves 4

478 cals   **11.2g** fat   **1.6g** saturates   **5.4g** sugars   **2g** salt

9oz clams
9oz mussels
¼ cup dry white wine
3 tablespoons extra-virgin
  olive oil
4 garlic cloves, sliced
½ teaspoon dried chile flakes
1 x 14.5oz can cherry tomatoes
salt
9oz defrosted langoustines,
  unpeeled
9oz uncooked jumbo shrimp,
  unpeeled
3 tablespoons chopped
  flat-leaf parsley
10oz linguine

1 Wash the clams and mussels under cold water. Discard any broken ones and any that do not close when tapped firmly.

2 Place the clams and mussels in a large saucepan, pour in the wine, and cook with the lid on for 3 minutes, until they have opened. Discard any that remain closed. Pour into a colander placed over a bowl to catch the juice and set aside.

3 Heat the oil in a large frying pan and gently fry the garlic until it begins to sizzle. Add the chile and the tomatoes and cook over medium heat for 5 minutes. Season with salt and stir occasionally.

4 Add ⅓ cup of the reserved cooking liquid from the mussels and clams and continue to simmer the sauce for 2 minutes.

5 Stir in the langoustines and the shrimp and continue to cook for another 3 minutes, until they turn pink.

6 Add the clams and mussels with the parsley and stir until heated through.

7 Meanwhile, cook the pasta in a large saucepan in plenty of boiling salted water, until al dente. Drain and pour into the pan with the sauce.

8 Toss everything together over low heat for 1 minute to allow all the flavors to coat the pasta. Serve immediately.

THE MISTAKE THAT PEOPLE OFTEN MAKE WITH THIS PASTA DISH is to use cooked shrimp instead of raw ones. The shrimp need to be raw so they can absorb the flavors of the garlic and the lemons and yet still be juicy and tender. Substitute the linguine with spaghetti if you like and make sure that you use a good-quality extra-virgin olive oil for the best flavor.

LINGUINE WITH GARLIC, SHRIMP & SPINACH
Linguine con gamberi e spinaci

serves 4

449 calories   **13.4g** fat   **1.9g** saturates   **4.2g** sugars   **0.9g** salt

10oz linguine
salt and freshly ground
  black pepper
¼ cup extra-virgin olive oil
1 garlic clove, sliced
5oz spinach leaves
14oz uncooked shrimp, peeled
¼ cup chopped flat-leaf parsley
grated zest of 1 lemon
10 cherry tomatoes, quartered

1 Cook the pasta in a large saucepan in plenty of boiling salted water, until al dente.

2 Meanwhile, in a large frying pan, heat the oil over medium heat and fry the garlic for 1 minute, until golden. Add the spinach and cook for another 2 minutes.

3 Add the shrimp with the parsley and season with salt and pepper. Stir well and continue to cook for 2 minutes.

4 Once the pasta is cooked, drain and add to the frying pan, then lower the heat.

5 Add the lemon zest and cherry tomatoes and stir everything together for 30 seconds. Serve immediately.

FOR ANYONE WHO IS LOOKING FOR A QUICK YET VERY TASTY PASTA DISH, this is definitely the one to try. I am a very big fan of roasted peppers in jars because they have a good flavor and you can use them any time. Make sure, once the pasta is cooked al dente, that you toss it together with the sauce, allowing the flavor of the sauce to coat it fully and evenly. If you prefer, you can use roasted peppers in oil, but drain them thoroughly.

PASTA WITH ROASTED PEPPERS, BASIL & GARLIC
Fettuccine con peperoni, basilico e aglio

serves 4

383 calories   **7.5g** fat   **1.1g** saturates   **9.6g** sugars   **1.2g** salt

2 tablespoons extra-virgin
   olive oil
1 garlic clove, sliced
1 x 1lb jar roasted red
   peppers in brine, drained
   and sliced
salt and freshly ground
   black pepper
10 basil leaves
12oz dried or fresh fettuccine

1 Heat the oil in a large nonstick frying pan over medium heat and fry the garlic for 30 seconds, until golden. Add the roasted peppers, stir, and cook for another 2 minutes. Season with salt and pepper.

2 Put 4 quarts of water in a large saucepan with 3 tablespoons salt and bring to a boil. Cook the pasta in boiling salted water, until al dente. To get that perfect "bite," cook the pasta for 1 minute less than instructed on the package.

3 Once the pasta is ready, drain, reserving 3 tablespoons of the cooking water. Put the pasta into the frying pan with the peppers and increase the heat to high. Scatter the basil over the top and pour in the reserved water. Toss everything together for 30 seconds to allow the sauce to coat the pasta evenly. Serve immediately.

I REALLY BELIEVE THAT THE BEST FROZEN VEGETABLE IN THE WORLD HAS TO BE PEAS. In my house and in my office, I always keep a big bag of frozen peas just in case I get a craving for them. I know that many chefs will disagree with me and say that you should eat peas only when they are in season, but I don't care. I feel strongly that if you cook them in the right way, frozen peas are just as good as fresh, and this is definitely the recipe to prove it.

LITTLE SHELL PASTA WITH PEAS, HAM & EGGS
Pasta e piselli

serves 4

494 calorie   **18g** fat   **6g** saturates   **8.2g** sugars   **3.1g** salt

2 tablespoons olive oil
2 onions, finely chopped
6oz sliced cooked lean ham,
  cut into small pieces
7oz frozen peas
1 teaspoon dried chile flakes
1¾ cups vegetable stock
9oz little pasta shells
2 eggs
¾ cup freshly grated Parmesan
salt

1 Heat the oil in a large saucepan over medium heat and fry the onions for about 5 minutes, until golden. Add the ham and continue to fry for another 2 minutes, stirring occasionally.

2 Add the peas and chile and continue to cook for 3 minutes, stirring occasionally.

3 Pour in the stock, lower the heat, and leave to simmer for 15 minutes with the lid half on.

4 Remove the lid and add the pasta. Stir well and continue to cook over low heat, uncovered, for about 8 minutes, until the pasta starts to soften. Stir every 2 minutes to keep it from sticking.

5 Once the pasta is cooked, crack in the eggs and continue to cook for another minute, stirring constantly.

6 Finally, add the Parmesan, taste, and add a little salt, if necessary. Stir together well and serve immediately.

BEING A PASTA LOVER, I COULD EAT PASTA EVERY DAY, but, of course, it's nice to create variations of it and this is one of my favorites. The idea for this recipe actually came when I had some leftover meat sauce and I thought that with a few eggs and some pasta it would make a great frittata. It's an excellent dish to eat cold and to take with you on picnics or to work. If you prefer, you can substitute the spaghetti with linguine or tagliatelle.

SPAGHETTI & GROUND BEEF FRITTATA WITH ARUGULA
Frittata di spaghetti con rucola

serves 6   **510** calories   **22.3g** fat   **7.5g** saturates   **7.6g** sugars   **1g** salt

3 tablespoons extra-virgin olive oil
1 medium onion, finely chopped
1 carrot, peeled and finely chopped
1lb extra-lean ground beef
1¾ cups tomato sauce
salt and freshly ground black pepper
10oz dried spaghetti
4 large eggs
¼ cup chopped flat-leaf parsley
½ cup freshly grated Parmesan
3oz arugula leaves

1 Heat 2 tablespoons of the oil in a large frying pan and fry the onion and carrot for 5 minutes, until soft, stirring occasionally.

2 Add the ground beef and continue to cook for another 5 minutes, stirring continuously until colored all over.

3 Pour in the tomato sauce, season with salt and pepper, and continue to cook over medium heat for 10 minutes, stirring occasionally.

4 Meanwhile, cook the pasta in a large saucepan in plenty of boiling salted water, until al dente. Drain and add to the pan with the meat sauce. Stir well and leave to cool. Preheat the oven to 350°F.

5 Break the eggs into the meat sauce and pasta in the pan and add the parsley and the grated Parmesan. Mix everything together well.

6 Brush a little oil over an 11in-diameter baking dish with sides about 2in high. Pour in the pasta mixture and spread out, ensuring it is all leveled beautifully.

7 Cook in the middle of the oven for 20 minutes, until crispy and set. Remove from the oven and allow to rest for 5 minutes.

8 Transfer the frittata to a serving plate and scatter the arugula on top. Serve warm or cold.

WHEN I WAS A YOUNG BOY, I remember that I used to go to my aunt's house after school and, religiously, once a week, she would prepare me this amazing dish. The Genovese sauce is very similar to the Bolognese sauce, except that there are no tomatoes involved, allowing you really to taste the ground beef. Believe me, once you have tried this pasta dish, it will become a regular in your weekly menu and you will be very popular with your friends! If you prefer, you can substitute the Pecorino Romano with freshly grated Parmesan cheese, but always use white onions.

PASTA WITH GROUND MEAT & ONIONS
Maccheroni alla Genovese

serves 4

615 calories **19.5g** fat **7.1g** saturates **10.9g** sugars **1.3g** salt

2 tablespoons olive oil
2 large onions, finely sliced
1 carrot, finely chopped
7oz extra-lean ground beef
3½oz lean ground lamb
⅓ cup white wine
salt and freshly ground
  black pepper
¾ cup vegetable stock
¼ cup chopped
  flat-leaf parsley
12oz macaroni
½ cup freshly grated
  Pecorino Romano

1 Heat the olive oil in a large saucepan over high heat and fry the onions and carrot for about 8 minutes, stirring occasionally, until softened and golden.

2 Add the beef and the lamb and mix well, allowing the ground meats to crumble. Continue to cook, stirring frequently, for about 10 minutes, until the meat has browned all over.

3 Pour in the wine and cook for 3 minutes, until evaporated. Season with salt and pepper and pour in the stock. Bring to a boil.

4 Lower the heat, add the parsley and simmer, uncovered, for 30 minutes, stirring occasionally.

5 Meanwhile, put 4 quarts of water in a large saucepan with 3 tablespoons salt and bring to a boil. Cook the pasta in the salted boiling water, until al dente. To get that perfect "bite," cook the pasta for 1 minute less than instructed on the package.

6 Drain the pasta and immediately add to the sauce. Increase the heat to high and mix the sauce and the pasta together for 30 seconds, stirring constantly, to allow the sauce to coat the pasta evenly.

7 Serve immediately with grated Pecorino on top.

I REALLY BELIEVE THAT GNOCCHI ARE VERY UNDERESTIMATED and, honestly, I do not understand why. These days, you can find ready-made gnocchi available to buy everywhere and, considering that they are so easy to cook, there really is no excuse not to try this recipe. When you buy gnocchi, make sure that you read the ingredients on the package, because what you are looking for is a gnocchi made with at least 70 percent potato. Also, make sure you always use fresh basil leaves and never the dried ones from jars.

GNOCCHI WITH TOMATO & BASIL SAUCE
Gnocchi al pomodoro e basilico

serves 4

301 calories **6.1g** fat **0.8g** saturates **10.7g** sugars **2.2g** salt

2 tablespoons extra-virgin olive oil
1 onion, finely chopped
2¼ cups tomato sauce
10 fresh basil leaves
salt and freshly ground black pepper
1lb ready-made plain gnocchi

1 Heat the oil in a large frying pan over medium heat and fry the onion for about 3 minutes, until golden.

2 Pour in the tomato sauce and continue to cook for another 10 minutes, stirring occasionally.

3 Stir in the basil, season with salt and pepper, and remove from the heat.

4 Meanwhile, fill a medium saucepan three-quarters full with water, add 1 tablespoon salt, and bring to a boil. Drop the gnocchi into the boiling water and leave until they start to float to the top. Drain and place in the frying pan with the sauce.

5 Return the frying pan to medium heat and cook for 2 minutes, stirring occasionally to allow the sauce to coat the gnocchi. Serve immediately.

OF COURSE, AS THE ITALIAN TITLE OF THIS RECIPE SUGGESTS, this pasta dish comes from the town of Sorrento, where, famously, gnocchi are made with mozzarella, basil pesto, and sieved tomatoes. I have added olives to give this dish a twist, but you can leave them out, if you prefer.

BAKED TOMATO GNOCCHI
Gnocchi alla Sorrentina

serves 4

514 calories **27.5g** fat **8.8g** saturates **6.6g** sugars **4.3g** salt

2 tablespoons extra-virgin olive oil
1 garlic clove, finely chopped
1¾ cups tomato sauce
4oz kalamata olives, pitted
4oz ready-made good-quality pesto Genovese (pesto made with basil and pine nuts)
salt and freshly ground black pepper
1lb ready-made plain gnocchi
1 mozzarella ball (4oz), drained and cut into small chunks

1 Heat the oil in a large nonstick frying pan over medium heat and fry the garlic for about 30 seconds. Pour in the tomato sauce and olives and continue to cook, stirring occasionally, for another 10 minutes.

2 Stir in the pesto, season with salt and pepper, and remove from the heat.

3 Meanwhile, fill a medium saucepan three-quarters full with water, add 1 tablespoon salt, and bring to a boil. Preheat the oven to 400°F.

4 Cook the gnocchi in the boiling water until they start to float to the top. Drain and place in the frying pan with the sauce.

5 Transfer to a baking dish. Scatter the mozzarella cheese over the top and place in the middle of the oven for 10 minutes. Serve hot.

WHEN PIZZA WAS CREATED IN NAPLES, THIS WAS THE ONLY TOPPING AVAILABLE at the time and it still remains probably the most requested by any Neapolitan. The marriage of anchovies, garlic, and olives is literally superb and, as far as I'm concerned, it's one of the best toppings ever made. It is very important to add the garlic 2 minutes before the pizza is ready, otherwise it will get burned and you will lose the sweet flavor. Never attempt to use anchovies that are marinated in vinegar for this recipe—those are only for salads and antipasti and not for pizza toppings.

PIZZA TOPPED WITH ANCHOVIES, GARLIC & BLACK OLIVES
Pizza alla marinara

makes 2 pizzas, serves 2

583 calories   **22.9g** fat   **3.3g** saturates   **10.7g** sugars   **5g** salt

pinch of salt
1 teaspoon dried yeast
½ cup warm water
1½ cups all-purpose flour, plus extra for dusting
1 tablespoon extra-virgin olive oil, plus extra for greasing

for the topping
1¾ cups tomato sauce
10 canned anchovy fillets in oil, drained
20 pitted black olives, halved
2 tablespoons extra-virgin olive oil
1 tablespoon dried oregano
salt and freshly ground black pepper
2 garlic cloves, sliced

1 To prepare the dough, mix the salt and yeast together in a measuring cup with the water. Place the flour in a large bowl, make a well in the center, and add the water mixture, along with the oil. Use a wooden spoon to mix everything together well to create a wet dough.

2 Turn out the dough onto a clean, well-floured surface and work it with your hands for about 5 minutes, or until smooth and elastic. Place in a greased bowl and cover with a kitchen towel. Leave at room temperature to rise for at least 30 minutes, until the dough has nearly doubled in size.

3 Meanwhile, preheat the oven to 425°F.

4 Turn out the dough onto a floured surface and divide it into two. Use your hands to push each out from the center, creating two rounds about 10in in diameter. Place the pizza bases on two oiled baking sheets.

5 Spread the tomato sauce on top of the pizza dough using the back of a tablespoon and season with salt and pepper.

6 Divide the anchovies and olives between the pizzas and drizzle with the extra-virgin olive oil. Sprinkle the oregano over the top and cook in the middle of the oven for about 20 minutes, or until the edges of the pizza are golden brown. Two minutes before the end of the cooking time, scatter the garlic on top of the pizzas. Serve hot.

ONE OF THE FIRST THINGS I LEARNED when I was in catering school was how to make a good focaccia. Please buy good-quality pesto, because it will make such a difference.

FOCACCIA WITH CHERRY TOMATOES & PESTO
Pizzaccia

serves 6

| **392** calories | **14.6g** fat | **2.4g** saturates | **2.6g** sugars | **0.7g** salt |

3½ cups all-purpose flour,
  plus extra for dusting
2 teaspoons dried yeast
½ teaspoon salt
5 tablespoons extra-virgin
  olive oil
1 cup warm water
10oz cherry tomatoes
salt and freshly ground
  black pepper
handful of fresh basil leaves
2 tablespoons ready-made,
  good-quality pesto Genovese
  (pesto made with basil and
  pine nuts)

1 Sift the flour into a large bowl, stir in the yeast, and add the salt. Make a well in the center, pour in 3 tablespoons of the oil and the water, and mix everything together with a wooden spoon. Transfer the mixture to a floured surface and knead for 10 minutes, until you create a smooth and elastic dough.

2 Place the dough in a greased bowl, cover with a clean kitchen towel, and leave to rise in a warm place for about 1 hour, until nearly doubled in size.

3 Oil a baking sheet measuring about 16 x 16in.

4 Punch down the dough and place on the oiled baking sheet. Stretch into a shape no more than   in thick. Leave to rest for 20 minutes. Preheat the oven to 450°F.

5 In a small bowl, mix together 3 tablespoons water with 1 tablespoon of the olive oil.

6 Once the 20 minutes are up, brush the stretched dough with the water and oil mixture and transfer the tray to the middle of the oven for about 20 minutes.

7 Meanwhile, quarter the cherry tomatoes. Place in a colander and sprinkle some salt over them, then set them aside for 10 minutes to allow any excess water to drain off.

8 Once the tomatoes are ready, place them in a bowl with the fresh basil and the pesto. Drizzle the remaining olive oil over the top and mix well. At this point, the focaccia should be ready: remove it from the oven and cover it with the cherry tomatoes and pesto mix. Serve immediately.

OFTEN PEOPLE HAVE THE MISCONCEPTION THAT MAKING YOUR OWN PIZZA IS EXTREMELY DIFFICULT. This is not the case; considering that very few things can go wrong. Once you make sure that the dough is made correctly and you have the right ingredients for the topping, the rest is just following my instructions. In the unlikely event that you don't get a good result the first time, please do not be put off. Try again—remember that practice makes perfect. It's vital to preheat your oven, otherwise your pizza can get soggy.

PIZZA TOPPED WITH MOZZARELLA, MUSHROOMS & HAM
Pizza Capricciosa

makes 2 pizzas, serves 4

434 calories **22.5g** fat **6.8g** saturates **5.7g** sugars **3.1g** salt

pinch of salt
1 teaspoon dried yeast
½ cup warm water
1½ cups all-purpose flour, plus extra for dusting
1 tablespoon extra-virgin olive oil, plus extra for greasing

for the topping
3 tablespoons extra-virgin olive oil
4oz button mushrooms, sliced
1¾ cups tomato sauce
1 teaspoon dried oregano
salt and freshly ground black pepper
1 mozzarella ball (4½oz), drained and cut into small cubes
20 pitted green olives, halved
6 slices of lean cooked ham, cut into strips
8 fresh basil leaves

1 To prepare the dough, mix the salt and yeast together in a measuring cup with the water. Place the flour in a large bowl, make a well in the center, and add the water mixture, along with the oil. Use a wooden spoon to mix everything together well to create a wet dough.

2 Turn out the dough onto a clean, well-floured surface and work it with your hands for about 5 minutes, or until smooth and elastic. Place in a greased bowl and cover with a kitchen towel. Leave at room temperature to rise for at least 30 minutes, until the dough has nearly doubled in size. Meanwhile, preheat the oven to 425°F.

3 Heat 1 tablespoon of the oil in a frying pan over medium heat and cook the mushrooms for 3 minutes, until tender, stirring occasionally.

4 Turn out the dough onto a floured surface and divide it into two. Use your hands to push out from the center, creating two rounds about 10in in diameter. Place the pizza bases on two oiled baking sheets.

5 Spread the tomato sauce on top of the dough using the back of a tablespoon. Sprinkle with the oregano and season with salt and pepper.

6 Divide the mozzarella, mushrooms, and olives between the pizzas and drizzle the remaining olive oil over the top. Cook in the middle of the oven for about 20 minutes, or until the edges of the pizza are golden brown. Two minutes before the end of the cooking time, scatter the ham and the basil over the top. Serve hot and enjoy your Capricciosa!

FOR ANYONE WHO HAS NEVER ATTEMPTED TO MAKE A RISOTTO, this is the recipe to start with. Make sure you toast the rice in the oil for at least 3 minutes, so the risotto will stay nice and al dente. If you can find them in season, replace the dried porcini with 6oz of fresh porcini mushrooms. In the unlikely event that you have any left over, remember, you can reheat rice only once and it will keep refrigerated for 48 hours. This is a great dish to take to the office for lunch the next day.

MUSHROOMS AND WHITE WINE RISOTTO
Risotto ai funghi

serves 4

511 calories **15.9g** fat **6g** saturates **2.5g** sugars **1.8g** salt

1oz sliced, dried porcini
    mushrooms
2 tablespoons olive oil
1 onion, finely chopped
4oz button mushrooms,
    sliced
3oz chestnut mushrooms,
    sliced
1 tablespoon fresh thyme
    leaves
12oz Arborio or Carnaroli rice
⅓ cup dry white wine
5 cups warm vegetable stock,
    made with 2 stock cubes
salt and freshly ground
    black pepper
2 tablespoons butter
½ cup freshly grated Parmesan

1 Soak the dried porcini mushrooms in cold water for 30 minutes. When they have softened, drain them.

2 Heat the olive oil in a large saucepan and fry the onion over medium heat for about 2 minutes, stirring occasionally, until softened.

3 Add all the mushrooms with the thyme and continue to cook for another 3 minutes, stirring occasionally.

4 Add the rice and stir continuously for 3 minutes, allowing the rice to toast in the olive oil and begin to absorb all the mushroom flavors.

5 Pour in the wine and continue to cook for another 3 minutes to evaporate the alcohol.

6 Start to add the warm stock a little at a time, stirring occasionally, allowing the rice to absorb the stock before adding more. Season well and cook gently (if you find you need extra liquid, use a little warm water).

7 After about 20 minutes, when most of the stock has been absorbed, remove the pan from the heat and stir the butter into the risotto. It is very important that you stir the butter very quickly into the rice for at least 30 seconds—this creates a fantastic creamy texture.

8 At the end, stir in the Parmesan and serve immediately.

IN THE EARLY SPRING OF 2009 I WENT TO VISIT A FRIEND OF MINE IN PISA. Pisa is an extremely good place for growing asparagus. My friend's mother prepared me the most beautiful asparagus and butternut squash risotto, and since then it has become one of my favorite risotto dishes. You can substitute the butternut squash with pumpkin if you wish, but never ever use canned asparagus.

BUTTERNUT SQUASH AND ASPARAGUS RISOTTO
Risotto con asparagi e zucca

serves 4

507 calories   **18.8g** fat   **6.7g** saturates   **6.9g** sugars   **2g** salt

3 tablespoons extra-virgin
   olive oil
1 medium onion, chopped
9oz Arborio or Carnaroli rice
¾ cup dry white wine
9oz butternut squash, peeled,
   deseeded, and cut into
   ½in cubes
2 thyme sprigs, leaves stripped
   and chopped
about 2½ cups warm vegetable
   stock
12 asparagus spears, chopped
   to about the same size as
   the squash
1 teaspoon butter
1 cup freshly grated Parmesan
salt and freshly ground
   black pepper

1   Heat the oil in a large saucepan and fry the onion until softened but not colored.

2   Add the rice and fry for 3 minutes over medium heat, allowing the rice grains to toast. Stir continuously using a wooden spoon.

3   Pour in the wine and continue to cook for a minute more before adding the squash and thyme. Pour in a couple of ladlefuls of the warm stock and bring to a simmer. Continue to cook and stir until all the stock is absorbed.

4   Pour in the rest of the stock a ladleful at a time and cook until each addition is absorbed. After 15 minutes, add the asparagus, and cook for 5 minutes.

5   Once the squash is soft and the rice cooked, remove the pan from the heat and add the butter and the Parmesan. At this point, stir everything for 1 minute to allow the risotto to become creamy. Season with salt and pepper and serve immediately.

IF I AM HONEST WITH YOU, THIS IS A LITTLE TRICKY, simply because there is a bit of preparation to do for the shellfish. Of course, like everything in life, if you put in the extra effort you will get the extra results. Make sure that the shrimp are raw, otherwise they will be tough and chewy. You can substitute the mussels with large clams but, whatever you do, never add Parmesan or any kind of cheese to a fish risotto.

SEAFOOD RISOTTO
Risotto di mare

serves 4

517 calories   **13.5g** fat   **4.2g** saturates   **2.4g** sugars   **2g** salt

6oz mussels
2 tablespoons olive oil
1 onion, finely chopped
12oz Arborio or Carnaroli rice
1 sachet (125mg) of saffron
  powder
⅓ cup dry white wine
5 cups warm fish stock,
  made with 2 fish stock cubes
salt and freshly ground
  black pepper
6oz uncooked shrimp, peeled
3½oz large scallops with the
  coral, halved
grated zest of 1 lemon
2 tablespoons butter
2 tablespoons chopped chives

1 Place the mussels in the sink and scrape off any grit under cold running water. Use your fingers to pull away the hairy beards that protrude from the shells. Tap any mussels that remain open with the back of a knife and discard them if they refuse to close. Rinse again in cold water until there is no trace of sand. Set aside.

2 Heat the olive oil in a large saucepan on medium heat and fry the onion for about 2 minutes, stirring occasionally, until softened.

3 Add the rice and stir continuously for 3 minutes, allowing the rice to toast in the olive oil.

4 Add the saffron and the wine and continue to cook for another 3 minutes to evaporate the alcohol.

5 Start to add the warm stock a little at a time, stirring occasionally, allowing the rice to absorb the stock before adding more. Season well and cook gently (if you find you need extra liquid, use a little warm water).

6 After about 13 minutes, just before most of the stock has been absorbed, add the shrimp, scallops, mussels, and lemon zest and continue to cook for another 7 minutes.

7 Remove the pan from the heat and stir the butter into the risotto. It is very important that you stir the butter very fast into the rice for at least 30 seconds—this creates a fantastic creamy texture.

8 At the end, stir in the chives and serve immediately.

MY BOYS LOVE THIS DISH. CHICKEN AND PEAS ARE ALWAYS A WINNER IN THEIR EYES and added to a risotto make an excellent meal. If you prefer, you don't have to add the white wine—you can replace it with more water or stock—and instead of rosemary you can use thyme leaves. Remember, never, ever cook a risotto with the lid on, because you should be stirring the rice continuously during cooking.

CHICKEN & PEA RISOTTO
Risotto con pollo e piselli

serves 4

594 calories **16.7g** fat **6.3g** saturates **3.4g** sugars **1.9g** salt

2 skinless, boneless chicken breasts
2 tablespoons olive oil
1 onion, finely chopped
1 tablespoon fresh rosemary leaves, finely chopped
12oz Arborio or Carnaroli rice
⅓ cup dry white wine
5 cups warm chicken stock, made with 2 stock cubes
salt and freshly ground black pepper
6oz frozen peas, defrosted
2 tablespoons butter
½ cup freshly grated Parmesan

1 Preheat the broiler until hot. Place the chicken breasts on a baking sheet and cook under the broiler for 3 minutes on each side. Cut into in cubes and set aside. (At this point, the chicken will not be fully cooked, but don't panic.)

2 Heat the olive oil in a large saucepan over medium heat and fry the onion for about 2 minutes, stirring occasionally, until softened. Add the rosemary and continue to cook for another 2 minutes, stirring occasionally.

3 Add the rice and stir continuously for 3 minutes, allowing the rice to toast in the olive oil and begin to absorb all the rosemary flavor.

4 Pour in the wine and continue to cook for another 3 minutes to evaporate the alcohol.

5 Start to add the warm stock a little at a time, stirring occasionally, allowing the rice to absorb the stock before adding more. Season well and cook gently (if you find you need extra liquid, use a little warm water).

6 After about 15 minutes, add the peas and the chicken, stir everything together, and continue to simmer for another 5 minutes over low heat until the rice and chicken are cooked.

7 Remove the pan from the heat and stir the butter into the risotto. It is very important that you stir the butter very fast into the rice for at least 30 seconds—this creates a fantastic creamy texture.

8 At the end, stir in the Parmesan and serve immediately.

fish
pesce

This was probably the easiest chapter for me to write since, coming from Naples and being brought up by the sea, I lived on all kinds of fish when I was younger. I find it quite amusing that many people are still scared of cooking fish, because it really is one of the easiest ingredients to work with. If I had to give anyone one main tip about fish recipes, it would be to make sure that they buy the freshest fish that they can get their hands on. It really does make a difference to the end result.

IF YOU ARE A STEAK TARTARE LOVER LIKE ME AND YET ALSO LOVE FISH, I have come up with a perfect recipe for you. Believe me when I tell you that if you serve this dish at a dinner party, your guests will be really impressed and inspired. The preparation of the salmon may be a little tricky for some, so an easier option would be to use sliced smoked salmon. Please make sure you buy good-quality olives and some good ciabatta bread.

SALMON & VEGETABLE TARTARE
Tartara di salmone e verdure

serves 4

616 calories   **32.8g** fat   **5.6g** saturates   **19.5g** sugars   **2.8g** salt

1lb salmon fillet
2 tablespoons sugar
2lb rock salt
1 avocado
juice of 1 lemon
2 celery sticks
1 large carrot
1 yellow pepper
10 cherry tomatoes, quartered
3 shallots, finely chopped
¼ cup chopped chives
10 pitted black olives, cut in quarters
salt and freshly ground black pepper
3 tablespoons extra-virgin olive oil
1 teaspoon prepared English mustard
8 thin slices of ciabatta, toasted

1 Place the salmon on a large serving plate and sprinkle the sugar over the top. Cover the fillet entirely with the rock salt and leave in the fridge to cure for at least 10 hours.

2 Once the salmon is ready, wash it under cold water, and use a long sharp knife to slice the fillet thinly.

3 Peel and pit the avocado and cut the flesh into small cubes (about ¹/₂in). Place in a small bowl and pour the freshly squeezed lemon juice over the top.

4 Cut the celery, carrot, and yellow pepper into cubes the same size as the avocado. Place in a large bowl with the cherry tomatoes, shallots, chives, and olives. Season with salt and pepper and drizzle the extra-virgin olive oil over the top.

5 Add the cubed avocado with the lemon juice, along with the mustard, to the cubed vegetables and gently mix everything together.

6 To serve, place a baking ring in the center of a serving plate. Cover the bottom of the ring with some of the vegetables and then cover with slices of salmon. Repeat the layers, ending with vegetables, and press down firmly. (You should have five layers, beginning and ending with vegetables and with two layers of salmon in the center.) Repeat the process for the other three plates.

7 Just before serving, remove the rings and serve with toasted warm ciabatta.

PINE NUTS ARE VERY UNDERESTIMATED AND VERSATILE. They are a natural source of fiber and of vitamin E. They complement the delicate taste of salmon perfectly. However, they are high in calories, so don't use too many. If you prefer, you can substitute the salmon with cod or even pink trout.

SALMON WITH PINE NUTS & LEMON THYME CRUST
Filetti di salmone con crosta di pinoli

serves 4

368 calories **24.2g** fat **3.4g** saturates **1g** sugars **0.6g** salt

2 tablespoons chopped lemon thyme
2 slices of white bread, torn into small pieces
grated zest of 1 lemon
¼ cup pine nuts
4 salmon fillets, about 4½oz each, skin on
salt and freshly ground black pepper
1 tablespoon extra-virgin olive oil

1 Preheat the broiler.

2 First, prepare the crust. Place the lemon thyme, white bread, lemon zest, and pine nuts in a food processor and process to make crumbs. Set aside.

3 Wash the salmon fillets and pat dry with paper towels. Lay the salmon on a baking sheet, skin-side up, and place under the broiler for 3 minutes. Turn them over and season with salt and pepper.

4 Divide the prepared crumbs between the four fillets and press down over the salmon flesh. Drizzle the oil on the top and put under the broiler for 3 minutes, taking care not to burn the crust. Reduce the oven temperature to 375°F.

5 Transfer to the middle of the oven for about 7–8 minutes, or until the salmon has cooked through. Serve right away.

Tip Don't let the salmon skin burn under the broiler, since it won't smell good!

IF EVER I'M HOME LATE FROM WORK OR I CAN'T BE BOTHERED TO COOK and yet want something really tasty that isn't difficult to prepare, this salmon recipe is certainly one of my first options. The combination of the tomatoes, garlic, and thyme is just sensational and it gives a really fresh taste without overpowering the flavor of the salmon. If you prefer, you can substitute the canned chopped tomatoes with canned cherry tomatoes, but you will definitely not be able to create the same sauce with fresh tomatoes. Also, try this recipe with fillet of sea bass or monkfish, since it works beautifully.

SALMON FILLETS IN TOMATO, GARLIC & THYME SAUCE
Salmone al pomodoro

serves 4

408 calories **25.5g** fat **4.2g** saturates **5.6g** sugars **0.6g** salt

2 tablespoons extra-virgin
    olive oil
3 garlic cloves, finely sliced
2 x 14.5oz cans chopped
    tomatoes
2 tablespoons fresh thyme
    leaves, chopped
salt and freshly ground
    black pepper
4 salmon fillets, about
    6oz each

1 Heat the oil in a medium frying pan and cook the garlic until it starts to sizzle. Add in the chopped tomatoes with the thyme, stir everything together, and bring to a boil. Season with salt and pepper and simmer for 8 minutes over medium heat, stirring occasionally.

2 Carefully slip the salmon into the sauce, cover with a lid, and cook for 4 minutes on each side. If the sauce is getting too thick, add a couple of tablespoons of water.

3 Remove the salmon from the pan and place on a large serving dish. Spoon the sauce over the fish and serve hot or warm.

THE PREPARATION FOR THIS DISH CAN BE DONE IN UNDER 4 MINUTES. Once you have blended the ingredients together, the job is then pretty much finished. You can even prepare it in the morning to cook in the evening. You can substitute the cod with monkfish or fillet of sea bass, but if you are not a fish lover, the recipe also works with chicken or pork chops.

FILLET OF COD WITH A SPICY RED PESTO
Merluzzo al pesto rosso piccante

serves 4

272 calories **10.1g** fat **1.2g** saturates **6.5g** sugars **1.9g** salt

1 x 14.5oz can chopped tomatoes
1 tablespoon extra-virgin
   olive oil
1 garlic clove
6oz sun-dried tomatoes in oil,
   drained
1 medium-hot red chile,
   deseeded
salt
4 cod fillets, about 6oz each
2 tablespoons chopped
   flat-leaf parsley

1 Preheat the oven to 375°F.

2 Place all the ingredients except the salt, cod, and parsley in a food processor and process until you create a smooth, creamy, and textured pesto. Taste and add a little salt if required.

3 Spoon the spicy red pesto on the top of each cod fillet (skin-side down if the cod comes with the skin). Place the fillets on a baking sheet and cook in the middle of the oven for 16 minutes.

4 Remove the baking sheet from the oven and let rest for 1 minute.

5 Serve each fillet of cod sprinkled with the parsley.

IN THE SUMMER OF 2008, I SPENT THREE WEEKS WITH MY FAMILY ON VACATION IN PORTUGAL and, let me tell you, if you like sardines, that is one of the only places on earth where you can find them cooked in every possible way. Personally, when I can find my sardines fresh, I prefer not to do much to them and not to use ingredients that will overpower their flavor. Capers, thyme, and fresh lemon are all you need to create a perfect sardine dish. Substitute the chopped thyme with rosemary, if you prefer, and make sure that you use a good-quality Italian extra-virgin olive oil.

FRESH SARDINES BAKED WITH LEMON & CAPERS
Sardine al limone e capperi

serves 4

233 calories   **16.7g** fat   **3.7g** saturates   **0.3g** sugars   **1.3g** salt

3 lemons
3 tablespoons extra-virgin olive oil
3 tablespoons chopped thyme
3 garlic cloves, sliced
3 tablespoons salted capers, rinsed
salt and freshly ground black pepper
12 fresh sardines, gutted

1 Preheat the oven to 375°F.

2 Grate the zest of 2 of the lemons onto a small plate and set aside. Squeeze the juice from the zested lemons and pour into a medium bowl. Pour in the oil, add the thyme, garlic, and capers, season with salt and pepper, and mix together thoroughly.

3 Place the sardines on a baking sheet and drizzle the dressing over the top. Cook in the middle of the oven for 25 minutes.

4 When the sardines are cooked, remove them from the oven and allow them to rest for 2 minutes.

5 Cut the remaining lemon into 4 wedges. Serve the sardines on a large serving platter, accompany with the lemon wedges, and sprinkle with the lemon zest. Serve hot or warm with your favorite salad.

PLEASE MAKE SURE THAT THE GRILL PAN IS VERY, VERY HOT, otherwise the fish will stick to it. Substitute the mackerel with sea bass, if you prefer.

BROILED FILLET OF MACKEREL WITH SUN-DRIED TOMATOES
Scombro grigliato con insalatina

serves 4

600 calories **44.7g** fat **8.8g** saturates **1.1g** sugars **0.9g** salt

1 tablespoon extra-virgin olive oil

2 tablespoons freshly squeezed lemon juice

1 teaspoon fennel seeds, crushed

pinch of dried chile flakes

salt and freshly ground black pepper

4 mackerel, about ¾lb each, cut into fillets (providing 8 fillets in total)

2oz arugula leaves

½ cup flat-leaf parsley

4 sun-dried tomatoes in oil, drained and finely sliced

1 tablespoon sherry vinegar

1 Pour the oil into a medium bowl with the lemon juice, fennel seeds, and chile flakes. Season with ¹/₂ teaspoon salt and a little black pepper. Mix everything together.

2 Brush some of the marinade on both sides of the mackerel fillets and leave to marinate on a plate for 10 minutes.

3 Meanwhile, mix the arugula leaves with the parsley and arrange in the middle of four serving plates.

4 Preheat a grill pan until very hot. Place the mackerel fillets on the grill pan, skin-side down, for 30 seconds. Turn and continue to cook the other side for another 30 seconds. Transfer the fillets to a plate.

5 Arrange the fish and sun-dried tomatoes over and around the arugula and parsley salad, trying not to flatten the leaves too much.

6 Preheat a medium frying pan and pour in the remaining marinade with the sherry vinegar. Mix and cook for 30 seconds.

7 Spoon the hot dressing over the salads and fish and serve immediately.

THIS RECIPE IS DEFINITELY A "WOW" DISH. The flavors are so clean and fresh and, I promise, you won't be hungry at the end of your meal. Please don't be frightened to cook fish. I know that many people find cooking a whole fish daunting, but this really is straightforward and completely worth it. If you prefer, you can make this dish with sea bream or whole salmon instead of sea bass.

BAKED WHOLE SEA BASS WITH TOMATOES, OLIVES & FENNEL

Spigola all'acqua pazza

serves 4

576 calories **16.1g** fat **4.9g** saturates **9.2g** sugars **3.8g** salt

2 tablespoons butter

1 large onion, finely sliced

1½lb potatoes (such as King Edward), peeled and cut into bite-sized chunks

5 large plum tomatoes, roughly chopped

1 large fennel bulb, thinly sliced

¾ cup dry white wine

¾ cup fish stock

4oz pitted green olives

⅓ cup capers in brine, drained and rinsed

2 whole sea bass, about 1¼lb each, gutted and scaled

salt and freshly ground black pepper

1 Preheat the oven to 400°F.

2 Melt the butter in a large heavy roasting pan on the stove and cook the onion gently for 5 minutes. Add the potatoes and mix well.

3 Add the tomatoes, half the sliced fennel, and the wine. Bring to a boil and cook until the liquid has been reduced to about half. Pour in the fish stock and add the olives and capers, stirring it all together well.

4 Use the remaining fennel to stuff the fish and place them on top of the vegetables. Spoon the vegetables and cooking juices over the fish and season well with salt and freshly ground black pepper.

5 Roast in the middle of the oven for 30 minutes.

6 When everything is cooked, place the two whole fish in the center of a large serving platter and scatter around the vegetables and juices.

IF YOU ARE NOT A MASSIVE FISH FAN, OUT OF ALL MY FISH RECIPES, I recommend you try this one. Not only is it the easiest to prepare, but it also has the least fishy flavor of all. Please make sure that once you have cooked the tuna you eat it right away, otherwise it can get tough and dry. You can also try this recipe with swordfish.

TUNA STEAK WITH GARLIC, OLIVE OIL & CHILE
Tonno aglio, olio e peperoncino

serves 4

445 calories **22.7g** fat **4.6g** saturates **0.1g** sugars **1.1g** salt

¼ cup extra-virgin
  olive oil
2 tablespoons water
1½ tablespoons freshly
  squeezed lemon juice
salt
1 garlic clove, finely chopped
1 tablespoon fresh oregano
  leaves, chopped
2 tablespoons capers in brine,
  rinsed and finely chopped
½ teaspoon dried chile flakes
2 tablespoons chopped
  flat-leaf parsley
4 tuna steaks, about 9oz each
  and 1in thick
arugula leaves

1 Preheat a grill pan until smoking hot, then reduce the heat to medium.

2 In a medium bowl, whisk the oil with the water until thick and creamy. Whisk in the lemon juice with a few pinches of salt. Stir in the garlic, oregano, capers, chile, and parsley.

3 Lightly brush the tuna steaks with the spicy dressing and cook on the grill pan for 2 minutes on each side.

4 Place a handful of arugula on four serving plates, then place a tuna steak on top each pile of leaves and drizzle the remaining spicy dressing over the top.

LENTILS ARE A VERY GOOD SOURCE OF IRON, PROTEIN, AND FIBER, and I think we all should make more of an effort to eat them as much as we can. I chose lentils for this recipe because they complement the shrimp really well, especially with the freshly squeezed lemon juice. It's a great dish for a main course, but do make sure that you buy good-quality shrimp. You can substitute the leeks with asparagus and if you really don't like lentils, try the recipe with canned chick peas.

JUMBO SHRIMP WITH LENTILS & LEEKS
Gamberoni con lenticchie e porri

serves 2

262 calories **9g** fat **1.3g** saturates **6.1g** sugars **1.6g** salt

2 leeks, cut into chunks
 1in long
8 uncooked jumbo shrimp,
 peeled
1 x 15.5oz can lentils
1 tablespoons extra-virgin
 olive oil
3 tablespoons freshly squeezed
 lemon juice
2 tablespoons pitted black
 olives, chopped
1 tablespoon chopped
 flat-leaf parsley
salt and freshly ground
 black pepper
2oz baby spinach leaves

1 Put the leeks into a steamer and steam for 8 minutes, then add the shrimp and continue to steam for 6 minutes more.

2 Meanwhile, drain the lentils and rinse under hot water. Place in a bowl and pour over the oil and the lemon juice. Add the olives and parsley, season with salt and pepper, and mix everything together.

3 Lift the leeks from the steamer and add to the bowl, along with the spinach. Mix again, check the seasoning, and divide between two serving plates.

4 Top the salad with the shrimp and drizzle any remaining dressing from the bowl over the top.

IF YOU ARE HAVING A DINNER PARTY BUT DON'T WANT TO SPEND TIME IN THE KITCHEN preparing your appetizer, this is the recipe for you. From start to finish, it will take no longer than 5 minutes and, therefore, give you plenty of time to entertain your guests. The flavors of my shrimp are so good that your guests will think that you have spent ages preparing them!

LEMON SHRIMP WITH GARLIC & BLACK PEPPER
Gamberoni aglio e limone

serves 4   **189** calories   **9.7g** fat   **1.4g** saturates   **1.1g** sugars   **0.8g** salt

1 large lemon
3 tablespoons olive oil
3 garlic cloves, finely chopped
2 fresh red chiles, sliced
20 jumbo shrimp,
   raw and unpeeled but
   with heads removed
5 tablespoons chopped flat-
   leaf parsley
salt and freshly ground
   black pepper
4 thin slices of ciabatta bread,
   toasted on both sides

1 Grate the zest of the lemon and set aside.

2 Heat the oil in a large frying pan over high heat. Add the garlic and chiles, then toss in the shrimp and fry for 4 minutes.

3 Cut the lemon in half and squeeze the juice from one half over the shrimp. Sprinkle the grated lemon zest and the parsley over the top. Toss everything together and continue to cook for another minute. Season with salt and plenty of black pepper.

4 Pile all the shrimp on a large serving platter and serve immediately accompanied by the toasted bread.

MUSSELS ARE BY FAR THE MAIN SHELLFISH THAT WE EAT IN NAPLES, therefore, as you can imagine, I have grown up eating mussels in many different ways. Traditionally, of course, we would never use heavy cream, but for this particular dish it works perfectly. If you buy saffron strands instead of the powder, please make sure that you grind before use. Never use red wine for this recipe.

QUICK MUSSEL STEW WITH SAFFRON & WHITE WINE
Cozze allo zafferano

serves 4

497 calories   **26.7g** fat   **10.2g** saturates   **4.6g** sugars   **2g** salt

3lb mussels

3 tablespoons extra-virgin olive oil

1 onion, finely chopped

⅓ cup white wine

⅓ cup heavy cream

3 tablespoons chopped flat-leaf parsley

1 sachet (125mg) saffron powder

salt and freshly ground black pepper

8 slices of ciabatta

1 Wash the mussels under cold water. Discard any broken ones and any that do not close when tapped firmly.

2 Heat the oil in a large saucepan and fry the onion for 2 minutes until softened.

3 Add the mussels, pour in the wine, and stir well. Cover the saucepan and cook over medium heat for 4 minutes.

4 Remove the lid, and pour in the cream with the parsley and the saffron. Season with salt and pepper, stir, and continue to cook for another 2 minutes, uncovered.

5 Once the sauce has thickened slightly, serve the mussels immediately with the sauce, discarding any that have not fully opened. Serve with some warm, crusty ciabatta.

meat
carne

Everybody knows that I am a massive meat lover, and here I have created for you some cool new recipes that will satisfy your culinary needs, make you look good if you serve them to your guests, and, yet, they are very simple to prepare. Better still, they are not loaded with calories, since they mostly use lean cuts of meat that are often combined with plenty of delicious vegetables.

THIS RECIPE IS A TYPICAL SUNDAY LUNCH FOR THE D'ACAMPO FAMILY. My boys absolutely love this dish and it doesn't take any time to prepare, so you can enjoy your weekend while your lunch/dinner is cooking. If you want to make the dish even healthier, discard the skin of the chicken before cooking and cover with some aluminum foil. My main tip is to get a good free-range chicken so the flavor will be so much better.

ROASTED CHICKEN WITH ROSEMARY & ZUCCHINI
Pollo al forno

serves 6

575 calories   **35.3g** fat   **9.4g** saturates   **5.9g** sugars   **0.6g** salt

1 large chicken, about 4½lbs
2 tablespoons rosemary leaves
2 tablespoons thyme leaves
10 garlic cloves, 6 peeled and 4 unpeeled
salt and freshly ground black pepper
3 carrots, cut into 1in chunks
3 zucchini, cut into 1in chunks
2 potatoes, peeled and cut into 1in chunks
2 tablespoons extra-virgin olive oil

1 Preheat the oven to 400°F.

2 Cut the chicken in half lengthwise using a sharp knife (straight down the middle of the breast and then down one side of the backbone) and make several cuts into the skin side.

3 Place the rosemary, thyme, and peeled garlic cloves on a cutting board and chop finely. Stuff the mixture into the cuts in the chicken skin and season all over with salt and pepper.

4 Place all the prepared vegetables with the unpeeled garlic in a roasting pan, drizzle half of the oil over the top, season with salt and pepper, and mix well.

5 Lay the chicken on top of the vegetables, skin-side up, drizzle with the remaining oil, and roast in the center of the oven for 35 minutes, basting the chicken with the cooking juices from the bottom of the pan after 15 minutes.

6 To check that the chicken is cooked, pierce each piece with a skewer: the juices should run clear.

7 Remove the chicken from the pan, cut each piece into three, and replace on top of the vegetables. Roast for another 8 minutes.

8 Remove the pan from the oven and rest for 3 minutes, allowing the meat to relax and become more tender.

9 To serve, place all the vegetables on a large serving dish, arrange the chicken pieces on top, and spoon any juices over the top.

AS YOU PREPARE THIS RECIPE, YOUR TASTEBUDS START WORKING OVERTIME. The smell from blending the ingredients together is amazing, and everyone will comment when entering your home while you are making it. Do not worry if the stuffing looks a little runny; actually, it will help to keep the chicken breast moist during cooking. If you don't like mushrooms, you can replace them with zucchini and instead of rosemary try some fresh thyme leaves. Trust me: you will love this recipe.

ROLLED BREAST OF CHICKEN STUFFED WITH MUSHROOMS & ROSEMARY
Rotolo di pollo ripieno ai funghi

serves 4

124 calories   **1.4g** fat   **0.4g** saturates   **2.7g** sugars   **0.4g** salt

4 skinless, boneless chicken breasts, about 4oz each
2 garlic cloves
1 carrot, chopped
4oz button mushrooms
1 large tomato, deseeded
1 tablespoon chopped rosemary leaves
salt and freshly ground black pepper
mixed greens, to serve

1 Preheat the oven to 400°F.

2 Place the chicken breasts between two sheets of plastic wrap on a cutting board. Use a meat mallet to beat out until about $1/4$in thick.

3 Place the rest of the ingredients in a food processor and season with salt and pepper. Process until you have a finely chopped and combined mixture.

4 Spread the mushroom mixture evenly on one side of the four chicken breasts. Roll up the breasts to encase the stuffing and secure with toothpicks.

5 Cut four squares of parchment paper and wrap up each chicken roll carefully. Place the parcels on a baking sheet and cook in the middle of the oven for 30 minutes, or until thoroughly cooked.

6 Unwrap the chicken rolls and remove the toothpick. Slice into rounds and serve with a fresh salad of your choice.

THIS RECIPE IS THE ULTIMATE ITALIAN WAY TO SERVE CHICKEN. Butter and lemon work perfectly with chicken and it couldn't be easier than this. Plus, who would have thought that this recipe had anything to do with calorie counting? It makes a great dinner for friends who are watching their weight and for those lucky ones who couldn't care less... they'll never know!

CHICKEN WITH LEMON BUTTER SAUCE
Pollo al limone

serves 4   **342** calories   **17.1g** fat   **8.7g** saturates   **0.6g** sugars   **1g** salt

**4 skinless, boneless chicken
  breasts
½ cup all-purpose flour
salt and freshly ground
  black pepper
1 tablespoon olive oil
5 tablespoons butter
¼ cup freshly squeezed
  lemon juice
¼ cup chicken stock
½ cup flat-leaf parsley, tough
  stalks removed, and finely
  chopped
mixed greens, to serve**

1   Place the chicken breasts on a cutting board and use a sharp knife to cut each one horizontally into two thin slices.

2   Put the flour onto a large plate, season with salt and pepper, and mix. Coat each side of the chicken breasts with the flour.

3   Heat the olive oil and half the butter in a large frying pan. Place the chicken in the pan and fry for 5 minutes on each side, until it starts to brown and is cooked through. (Work in batches, if necessary.)

4   Remove the chicken with a slotted spoon and keep it warm while you make the sauce.

5   Pour the lemon juice and the stock into the frying pan, scraping all the brown bits from the edges and bottom into the liquid. Bring to a boil, stirring for about 1 minute.

6   Add the chopped parsley and remaining butter and stir the mixture well to create a creamy texture.

7   Place two slices of chicken in the middle of each serving plate and drizzle the lemon sauce over the top. Serve with your favorite salad.

THIS DISH TAKES ME BACK TO MY CHILDHOOD, WHEN I WOULD COME HOME FROM SCHOOL and a fabulous smell would greet me. One-pot cooking is such a great way to bring together different flavors and colors. It is almost impossible to go wrong and, best of all, there aren't many dishes to do afterward!

BRAISED CHICKEN BREASTS WITH PEPPERS & ZUCCHINI
Pollo alla Torrese

serves 4

351 calories **12.3g** fat **1.7g** saturates **17.4g** sugars **0.7g** salt

2 tablespoons olive oil

4 skinless, boneless chicken breasts

salt and freshly ground black pepper

2 garlic cloves, finely chopped

2 tablespoons chopped rosemary leaves

1 red pepper, deseeded and sliced

1 yellow pepper, deseeded and sliced

zest and juice of 1 lemon

2 zucchini, thinly sliced into rounds

¼ cup slivered almonds

1oz raisins

2 x 14.5oz cans chopped tomatoes

1 Preheat the oven to 325°F.

2 Heat 1 tablespoon of the oil in a heavy-bottomed baking dish.

3 Cut the chicken breasts in half lengthwise, season with salt and pepper, and add to the hot oil. Gently fry on both sides, just until they start to color; do not cook the chicken through. (Work in batches, if necessary.) Remove the chicken and set aside.

4 Heat the remaining oil and gently fry the garlic, rosemary, and peppers for about 5 minutes, stirring occasionally.

5 Add the rest of the ingredients, season with a little salt and pepper, and return the chicken to the baking dish. Stir everything together.

6 Bring to a boil, then cover the baking dish, and place in the middle of the oven for 45 minutes. Serve hot.

THIS RECIPE COMES FROM THE TOWN OF PARMA, where prosciutto and Parmesan cheese are produced. I was there over Christmas 2008 and I saw this recipe served in a very famous restaurant and I thought I would share it with you. Of course, I added a few Gino twists with the mozzarella and oregano. If you are looking for a recipe will big, full flavor, this is the one!

CHICKEN BREAST WITH PARMESAN, TOMATOES & MOZZARELLA
Petto di pollo alla Parmigiana

serves 6

349 calories   **16.7g** fat   **6g** saturates   **6.7g** sugars   **1g** salt

3 eggplants, about 7oz each, cut lengthwise into ¼in slices
4 tablespoons olive oil, plus extra for brushing
1 egg, beaten
2 tablespoons skim milk
⅔ cup freshly grated Parmesan
⅔ cup bread crumbs, toasted
6 skinless, boneless chicken breasts, about 3½oz each
1 large onion, finely sliced
1 x 14.5oz can chopped tomatoes
1 teaspoon dried oregano
3½oz mozzarella, drained and sliced
salt and freshly ground black pepper

1 Preheat the broiler.

2 Pour 2 quarts water into a large saucepan with 1 teaspoon salt and bring to a boil.

3 Cook the eggplants in the boiling water for 2 minutes and drain. Allow to cool slightly, then pat dry with paper towels and place on a baking sheet. Brush with a little oil and cook under a hot broiler for 2 minutes on each side, until browned. Decrease the oven temperature to 350°F.

4 Mix the egg and milk together. Mix the Parmesan and bread crumbs together. Dip each chicken breast in the egg mixture and then coat with the Parmesan bread crumbs.

5 Heat 2 tablespoons of the olive oil in a large frying pan and cook the coated breasts for 2 minutes on each side, until colored. Drain on paper towels.

6 Heat the remaining olive oil in a medium saucepan and fry the onion for 5 minutes, stirring occasionally. Add in the tomatoes with the oregano and season with salt and pepper. Stir everything together and continue to cook for another 5 minutes.

7 Spoon the tomato mixture into a 2-quart shallow oven-proof dish and place the chicken breasts on top. Cover with overlapping layers of eggplant and mozzarella and then top with any remaining Parmesan bread crumbs.

8 Cook, uncovered, in the center of the oven for 35 minutes, until golden brown. Serve hot.

PORK LOIN WITH WHITE WINE & SAGE PESTO

Scaloppine di maiale al pesto di salvia This is the ultimate pork sandwich with a twist: there is no bread, the pork loins are the base and the filling is a sage pesto—amazing!

serves 4

428 calories   **29.7g** fat   **5g** saturates   **0.8g** sugars   **0.5g** salt

25 sage leaves
¼ cup peeled almonds
1 garlic clove
½ cup freshly grated Pecorino
5 tablespoons extra-virgin
    olive oil
16 slices of lean pork loin, each
    slice about 3½in in diameter
    and ¼in thick
salt and freshly ground
    black pepper
⅓ cup white wine
mixed greens, to serve

1 Wash the sage leaves and place in a food processor with the almonds, garlic, cheese, and 2 tablespoons of the oil. Process for 20 seconds to create a smooth sage pesto.

2 Use a sharp knife to make small cuts on the edges of the pork slices to prevent them from curling when you cook them.

3 Spread the sage pesto on eight of the slices of pork and cover with the remaining eight, creating a sandwich effect.

4 Heat the remaining oil in a large frying pan and fry the pork "sandwiches" on one side for 2–3 minutes. Turn the meat over and continue to cook for another 2 minutes. Season with salt and pepper.

5 Pour in the wine and continue to cook for 4 minutes, turning the meat at least once more. Serve immediately, allowing two "sandwiches" per portion and accompany with your favorite crispy salad.

PORK STEAKS WITH MUSHROOMS & ROSEMARY

Bistecche di maiale con funghi e rosmarino I often find pork steaks a bit boring, but the combination of the rosemary, orange juice, and mushrooms takes the flavor of the pork to another level, and with the kick of the chile—it has the perfect balance.

serves 4

209 calories   **10g** fat   **2.3g** saturates   **1.4g** sugars   **0.4g** salt

2 tablespoons olive oil
4 lean pork steaks (about
    4½oz each)
9oz button mushrooms,
    quartered
2 tablespoons chopped
    rosemary leaves
½ teaspoon dried chile flakes
juice of 1 large orange
1 tablespoon red wine vinegar
salt

1 Heat the oil in a large frying pan and fry the pork for 2 minutes on each side, until browned. Remove from the pan and set aside.

2 Add the mushrooms and rosemary to the frying pan and fry for 3 minutes, stirring occasionally.

3 Sprinkle the chile over the top and pour in the orange juice and the vinegar. Bring to a boil. At this point, return the pork steaks to the pan and cook over medium heat for 5 minutes to allow the meat to finish cooking and the sauce to thicken. Turn the pork halfway through. Season with salt and serve immediately.

THIS IS DEFINITELY THE PERFECT RECIPE FOR THOSE OF YOU WHO HAVE VERY LITTLE TIME, yet always have friends/family over for dinner. You can prepare the *crespelle* 24 hours before you actually cook them and you can substitute ground pork with beef or chicken, if you prefer. Whatever you do, make sure you serve them hot.

STUFFED CREPES WITH GROUND PORK & PARMESAN
Crespelle di maiale

serves 8

244 calories   **11.2g** fat   **3.8g** saturates   **7g** sugars   **0.4g** salt

1 cup all-purpose flour
1 egg
1 cup skim milk
3 tablespoons olive oil
2 onions, chopped
6oz button mushrooms, chopped
¾lb ground pork
4 sage leaves, finely chopped
1 x 14.5oz can tomatoes
salt and freshly ground black pepper
4 large round tomatoes, sliced
½ cup freshly grated Parmesan
mixed greens, to serve

1 Prepare the batter for the crepes by sifting the flour into a bowl. Make a well in the center and add the egg, with 2 pinches of salt. Whisk with a balloon whisk and gradually beat in the milk, drawing in the flour from the sides to make a smooth batter. Cover and leave to stand for 20 minutes.

2 Heat 2 tablespoons of the oil in a large frying pan and fry the onions for 3 minutes, until soft but not colored. Add the mushrooms and continue to fry for 2 minutes, stirring occasionally.

3 Add the ground pork, sage, and canned tomatoes to the frying pan and cook for another 15 minutes. Stir often, crumbling the meat as you do so. Season with salt and pepper and leave to cool at room temperature. Preheat the oven to 350°F.

4 To prepare the crepes, heat the remaining oil in an 8in heavy-bottomed pancake pan or frying pan. Pour in just enough batter to cover the bottom of the pan thinly and cook over medium heat for 1 minute, until golden brown. Turn and cook the other side for another 30 seconds, until golden. Transfer the crepe to a plate and keep warm while cooking the remaining seven.

5 Place the crepes on a flat surface. Divide the meat mixture evenly and place a portion in the center of each crepe. Roll up the crepes to encase the stuffing. Transfer the stuffed crepes to a baking sheet and place the sliced tomatoes on top. Sprinkle with the Parmesan.

6 Bake in the middle of the oven for 15 minutes, until beautifully crispy. Serve hot with your favorite green salad.

FOR ANYONE WHO LOVES MEATBALLS, THIS IS THE RECIPE FOR YOU. I chose lamb because it has so much flavor, especially when combined with onion and chile. If you are not a big fan of spicy dishes, you can substitute the red chile with drained sun-dried tomatoes. Please make sure that you use fresh rosemary leaves—the dried ones are garbage!

SPICY LAMB MEATBALLS WITH ONIONS & ROSEMARY
Polpettine di agnello

serves 4

354 calories **26.3g** fat **8.6g** saturates **2.3g** sugars **0.4g** salt

3 tablespoons olive oil, plus extra for brushing
1 onion, finely chopped
1 red chile, deseeded and finely chopped
1lb lean ground lamb
1 teaspoon paprika
2 tablespoons rosemary leaves, finely chopped
1 lemon
flour, for dusting
salt
mixed greens, to serve

1 Heat 1 tablespoon of the olive oil in a medium frying pan and cook the onion and chile over medium heat for 3 minutes, stirring occasionally, until softened. Allow to cool.

2 Put the ground lamb, paprika, rosemary, and cooled onion and chile mixture in a large bowl. Grate the zest of the lemon over the top and pour in half the juice. Season with salt and mix thoroughly. Cover with plastic wrap and leave to rest in the fridge for at least 8 hours.

3 When you are ready to cook, preheat the broiler to hot. Lightly flour the palms of your hands and shape the meat mixture into 28 balls.

4 Place the meatballs on a baking sheet and brush each one with a little oil. Cook under the broiler for 10 minutes, turning the meatballs frequently.

5 Divide the meatballs between four serving plates and accompany with a salad of your choice.

YOU MAY THINK THAT I'M GOING CRAZY BY PUTTING A BURGER RECIPE IN A DIET BOOK, but please trust me... my Italian burgers are full of healthy flavors and, therefore, you don't need a lot to be completely satisfied. You can substitute thyme leaves with fresh rosemary if you wish, and if you don't like sun-dried tomatoes you can use chopped green olives.

ITALIAN-STYLE BURGERS WITH SUN-DRIED TOMATOES & PARMESAN

serves 4

487 calories **23.5g** fat **8g** saturates **2.1g** sugars **1.7g** salt

1lb extra-lean ground beef
2 teaspoons thyme leaves, finely chopped
½ cup fresh bread crumbs
1oz sun-dried tomatoes in oil, drained and finely chopped
1 garlic clove, finely chopped
⅓ cup freshly grated Parmesan
salt and freshly ground black pepper
1 egg, beaten
1 tablespoon flour, for dusting
2 tablespoons olive oil, for brushing
2 hamburger buns
2½ cups mixed greens

1 Mix the ground beef, thyme, bread crumbs, sun-dried tomatoes, garlic, and Parmesan together in a large bowl. Season with salt and pepper and pour in the beaten egg to bind the mixture.

2 Lightly flour the palms of your hands and shape the meat mixture into four balls. Gently press each ball between your hands to create a burger shape. Brush each one with a little oil.

3 Preheat a grill pan until very hot and cook the burgers for 4 minutes on each side.

4 Meanwhile, warm the hamburger buns. When the burgers are ready, divide the mixed greens between the open buns, and top each half with a hot burger. Enjoy!

OFTEN PEOPLE HAVE THE MISCONCEPTION that you can only make meat skewers in the summer and cook them on a barbecue—but this is not the case. Make sure, once the skewers are ready to be cooked, that your grill pan is very, very hot so that the meat doesn't stick to the pan. Use sirloin steak if you prefer, and if you don't like mushrooms substitute them with baby onions.

SKEWERED MARINATED LAMB WITH ROSEMARY & MINT
Spiedini di agnello

serves 2

203 calories   **8.2g** fat   **3.6g** saturates   **8.7g** sugars   **0.9g** salt

6oz low-fat plain yogurt
1 tablespoon ready-made
  mint sauce
1 tablespoon chopped
  rosemary leaves
salt and freshly ground
  black pepper
6oz lean lamb, cut into
  1in cubes
6 medium button mushrooms
1 small red onion, quartered

1   Have ready four metal or wooden skewers—if you are using wooden ones, soak them in water beforehand, otherwise they will burn.

2   Mix together the yogurt, mint sauce, and rosemary in a large bowl and season with salt and pepper. Add the lamb and mix well to make sure that each piece is coated with the marinade. Leave to marinate at room temperature for 10 minutes.

3   Preheat a grill pan until hot or, if you prefer, preheat a barbecue. Thread the lamb onto the four skewers, alternating each piece with mushrooms and onion pieces.

4   Cook the lamb on the grill pan or barbecue for 3–4 minutes, turning the skewers to ensure that each side is colored. Serve hot.

UNFORTUNATELY, THIS RECIPE WILL NOT WORK WITH RED WINE, but you can definitely substitute the Gorgonzola with any blue cheese. This is the ultimate "minimum effort, maximum satisfaction" recipe.

SIRLOIN STEAK WITH GORGONZOLA & PINK PEPPERCORN SAUCE

Bistecca al Gorgonzola

serves 4

353 calories	**22.5g** fat	**11.9g** saturates	**0.2g** sugars	**1.4g** salt

2 tablespoons butter
1 tablespoon olive oil
4 sirloin steaks, about 4oz each
1 tablespoon pink peppercorns
⅓ cup white wine
3½oz Gorgonzola, cut into small cubes

1 Melt the butter with the oil in a large nonstick frying pan over high heat. Add the steaks and the peppercorns and cook the steaks for 3 minutes on each side. Do not season with salt.

2 Transfer the steaks to a plate, cover with foil, and keep warm while preparing the sauce. Leave the peppercorns in the frying pan. Pour the wine into the frying pan and leave to sizzle over high heat for 1 minute, stirring with a wooden spoon.

3 Lower the heat to medium and add the Gorgonzola cubes to the frying pan. Stir constantly with the spoon for 3 minutes, allowing the cheese to melt and create a smooth sauce. Place a steak in the middle of each serving plate and drizzle the Gorgonzola and peppercorn sauce on top.

FOR ANYONE WHO IS ON A DIET OR WATCHING THEIR DAILY CALORIE INTAKE, venison has to be the perfect meat to eat. It is very lean and yet very tasty. Unfortunately, we do not eat a lot of venison in the south of Italy, since it is more of a northern Italian ingredient, but every time I do eat it, I make it this way. Be sure to choose a good-quality red wine and marinate the meat for at least 5 hours.

VENISON MEDALLIONS IN RED WINE
Cervo al vino rosso

serves 6

266 calories   **7.7g** fat   **2.9g** saturates   **4.7g** sugars   **0.4g** salt

6 venison medallions, about
   6oz each
1 onion, finely chopped
2 tablespoons rosemary leaves
2 bay leaves
1 cup red wine
1 tablespoon butter
1 tablespoon olive oil
salt and freshly ground
   black pepper
2 tablespoons red currant jelly

1 Place the venison in a large, shallow, nonmetallic dish and scatter the onion, rosemary, and bay leaves over the top. Pour in the wine, cover with plastic wrap, and leave to marinate in the fridge for at leaat 5 hours. Turn the venison every hour to allow all the flavors to combine.

2 Remove the venison from the dish and reserve the marinade.

3 Heat the butter and the oil in a large frying pan over medium heat. Add the venison and cook for 4 minutes on each side. Season with salt and pepper. Transfer to a plate, cover with foil, and keep warm while preparing the sauce.

4 Strain the reserved marinade into the frying pan and bring to a boil. Use a wooden spoon to stir in the red currant jelly. Season with salt and pepper and cook for another 3 minutes, allowing the sauce to thicken slightly.

5 Arrange the medallions on a large serving dish and pour the red wine sauce over the top. Serve hot.

I HAVE TO ADMIT, I LOVE ANY KIND OF STEW. They are so easy to put together and the slow cooking makes all the ingredients taste fantastic. This is a recipe you can prepare 24 hours in advance, since that will only enhance the flavors. You can certainly use lamb if you prefer, and if you can't find diced pancetta, a good-quality bacon will definitely do the trick. I have tried this recipe with chicken or vegetable stock and both work just as well. Whatever you do, make sure the oven is preheated, and once the stew is out of the oven, let it rest for a good 10 minutes to allow the sauce to thicken.

SPICY BEEF & WILD MUSHROOM STEW
Stufato di manzo

serves 4

315 calories   **16g** fat   **5.2g** saturates   **6.3g** sugars   **1.4g** salt

**14oz lean rump roast, cut
   into 1in cubes**
1 tablespoon all-purpose flour
**2 tablespoons extra-virgin
   olive oil**
7oz baby onions
2oz pancetta, diced
**6oz mixed wild
   mushrooms, cleaned and
   roughly sliced**
**1 large carrot, cut into
   ½in cubes**
2 garlic cloves, finely chopped
½ cup red wine
1 tablespoon tomato paste
1½ cups beef stock
3 rosemary sprigs
1 bay leaf
**salt and freshly ground
   black pepper**

1 Preheat the oven to 400°F.

2 Place the cubed beef in a large bowl and dust with the flour.

3 Heat the oil in a large nonstick flame-proof baking dish and gently fry the beef for 2–3 minutes, until browned all over. Work in batches, if necessary. Remove from the pan and set aside.

4 Add the onions and pancetta to the pan and cook for 5 minutes, stirring occasionally. Add the wild mushrooms, carrot, and garlic and continue to cook for another 5 minutes. Pour in the wine and bring to a boil.

5 Return the beef to the pan, stir in the tomato paste, and gently mix together well. Pour in the stock a little at time, stirring as you do so, to create a sauce. Bring to a boil.

6 Tuck in the rosemary and the bay leaf, cover the baking dish and transfer to the middle of the oven for 25 minutes. Remove the lid for the last 5 minutes to allow the sauce to thicken.

7 Before serving, season with salt and pepper, and allow the baking dish to rest, out of the oven, for 10 minutes.

desserts
dolci

I bet you never thought that a dessert section would be in a diet book... it just goes to show how boring some diets can be and why people have trouble sticking to them. In this chapter you will find many delicious desserts that still give you the sweet fix that you are looking for, without piling on tons of calories. I like to use lots of fresh fruits as a starting point—in addition to satisfying a sweet tooth, they add lots of vitamins and minerals to your diet and count toward your "five-a-day."

THIS IS DEFINITELY AN ADULT VERSION OF A CHILDHOOD FAVORITE. Gelatin is a very retro dessert and quite rightly has re-earned its place on every dessert cart. For those not calorie counting, serve with ice cream for old time's sake!

SUMMER BERRIES & SWEET WINE GELATIN
Gelatina di frutta e vino dolce

serves 8

177 calories   **0.1g** fat   **0g** saturates   **36.7g** sugars   **0g** salt

8 sheets of gelatin or
   8 envelopes granulated
   gelatin
1¼ cups superfine sugar
1 cup water
1 cup sweet white dessert
   wine
1lb 10oz frozen summer
   berries, defrosted

1 Place the sheets (or envelopes) of gelatin in a small bowl, cover with water, and let soak for about 5 minutes, until soft.

2 Put the sugar in a heavy-bottomed saucepan with the water and heat gently until the sugar has dissolved. Increase the heat and let it boil for about 5 minutes, stirring occasionally, until a syrup forms. Remove from the heat.

3 Drain the softened gelatin into a sieve and add it to the syrup, stirring until the gelatin has dissolved. Pour in the wine and stir. Cool for about 15–20 minutes.

4 Take eight large wine glasses and add a layer of berries and gelatin in each, set in the fridge for 2 hours, and then add another layer of berries and gelatin and set for another 2 hours. Serve chilled.

I CHALLENGED MY GOOD FRIEND ALI SHALSON TO DEVISE A CHOCOLATE SAUCE suitable for someone who is calorie counting. She concocted this gorgeous butterscotch sauce, so I decided to serve it with my caramelized peaches because they complement each other really beautifully. So here it is... a chocolate dessert for those on a diet!

BROILED VANILLA PEACHES WITH BUTTERSCOTCH SAUCE
Pesche grigliate con salsa di cioccolato

serves 4

220 calories   **8.6g** fat   **5.4g** saturates   **34.1g** sugars   **0.8g** salt

½ vanilla pod
2 tablespoons brown sugar
2 tablespoons freshly squeezed lemon juice
4 peaches, quartered and pitted

for the butterscotch sauce
½ tablespoon cocoa powder
½ tablespoon cornstarch
½ cup skim milk
3 tablespoons butter
2 tablespoons brown sugar
½ teaspoon sea salt
1 tablespoon maple syrup

1   Preheat the broiler.

2   Slit the vanilla pod and scrape the seeds into a small bowl by running the back of a pointed knife down the pod. Add the brown sugar and lemon juice and mix together.

3   Arrange the peaches, cut-side up, on a baking sheet and brush with all the vanilla, lemon, and sugar syrup. Place under the broiler for about 5 minutes, until caramelized and the edges are starting to brown.

4   Meanwhile, prepare the sauce by sifting the cocoa powder and cornstarch into a little bowl and blending to a paste with a few teaspoons of the milk.

5   Heat the rest of the milk in a small nonstick saucepan, together with the butter, sugar, salt, and maple syrup. Keep stirring over low heat until the butter has melted and the sugar dissolved. Add the cocoa paste, stirring continuously, until it starts to bubble. Let it bubble for about 30 seconds to allow the sauce to thicken.

6   Place the peaches on a serving dish and drizzle any syrup that has collected in the baking sheet over the top.

7   Pour the butterscotch sauce into a small bowl and serve with the peaches. Enjoy!

ROASTED FRESH FRUITS WITH GRAND MARNIER

Frutta fresca al forno At the beginning of 2008 I spent two weeks in Tuscany searching for new ideas. I ate this dish when I was dining at my friend's house and I thought it would be a great recipe to include. It is so simple that I challenge anyone to mess it up. If you have any left over, you can always add yogurt to it and have it for breakfast—waste not, want not! Make sure that the fruits you're using are ripe but firm, otherwise the dish will be soggy.

serves 4

128 calories **0.3g** fat **0.1g** saturates **24.8g** sugars **0g** salt

2 pears, quartered lengthwise and cored

2 plums, halved and pitted

4 fresh figs, halved

2 peaches, quartered and pitted

juice of 2 oranges

3 tablespoons Grand Marnier

1 Preheat the oven to 400°F.

2 Place the pears, plums, figs, and peaches in a single layer in a roasting pan. Squeeze the juice from the orange over them and bake in the center of the oven for 18 minutes.

3 Remove the pan from the oven and pour the Grand Marnier over the fruit. Bake for another 6 minutes.

4 Divide the roasted fruits between four serving bowls and serve hot or warm.

STRAWBERRIES WITH AMARETTO & YOGURT

Insalata di fragole e amaretto We are all guilty of buying strawberries out of season and, of course, we are always disappointed since the flavor just isn't there. This is a fantastic way to bring them to life. If you prefer, substitute the Amaretto with Limoncello and instead of fresh mint, try fresh basil.

serves 4

143 calories **1g** fat **0.5g** saturates **25.6g** sugars **0.2g** salt

1¾lbs strawberries

3 tablespoons amaretto liqueur

1 tablespoon honey

11oz plain low-fat yogurt

4 fresh mint leaves, to decorate

1 Wash the strawberries under cold running water, drain, and dry well with paper towels. Hull the strawberries and cut them in half. Place in a large bowl, pour in the amaretto, and drizzle with the honey. Mix well and leave to marinate for 15 minutes at room temperature, stirring occasionally.

2 Divide the yogurt between four dessert glasses and spoon in the marinated strawberries. Drizzle with the remaining juices from the marinade and decorate with the fresh mint leaves before serving.

EVERY TIME I GO TO SORRENTO IN THE SOUTH OF ITALY, this is one of the first things that I crave. The lemons there are to die for, but, trust me, this sorbet works with any decent-quality lemon. It could also be used in between courses (especially between fish and meat). It cleanses the palate and is really refreshing.

FRESH LEMON SORBET
Sorbetto al limone

serves 6   **70** calories **0g** fat **0g** saturates **18.5g** sugars **0g** salt

2 limes
1 quart cold water
½ cup superfine sugar
1¼ cups freshly squeezed lemon juice

1 Finely grate the zest from the limes and set aside.

2 Squeeze the juice from the limes and place in a medium saucepan with the water.

3 Add the sugar and the lime zest to the saucepan and simmer, stirring occasionally, until the sugar has dissolved.

4 Remove from the heat, stir in the lemon juice, and allow to cool. Pour into a shallow freezer-proof container and freeze until crystals form around the edges.

5 Remove from the freezer, stir the mixture vigorously with a fork, then return it to the freezer. Repeat this process every 20 minutes over the next few hours until no liquid remains in the container.

6 Remove the sorbet from the freezer to soften slightly before serving to make it easier to scoop out.

STRAWBERRIES SCREAM SUMMER, but you can use any fruit of your choice in these beautiful little pastry treats. Remember that being on a diet doesn't mean going without. Substitutions can easily be made in recipes, including this one, which I originally made with whipped heavy cream and several more layers of pastry.

STRAWBERRY FILO TARTS WITH BASIL CRÈME FRAÎCHE
Tartine di fragole e basilico

serves 4

179 calories **10.6g** fat **5.5g** saturates **8.1g** sugars **0.3g** salt

¾oz unsalted pistachio nuts
⅓ cup 2% crème fraîche
grated zest of lemon
3 tablespoons confectioners' sugar, sifted
4 basil leaves, shredded, plus 4 small basil sprigs to decorate
4 sheets of filo pastry
1½ tablespoons butter, melted
4oz strawberries, quartered

1 Preheat the oven to 375°F.

2 First put the pistachio nuts into a small sandwich bag and crush using a rolling pin.

3 Place the crème fraîche into a small bowl and mix in two-thirds of the crushed pistachio nuts, half the lemon zest, half the confectioners' sugar, and the shredded basil leaves. Set aside.

4 Lay out a sheet of filo pastry and brush with the melted butter. Sprinkle a third of the remaining pistachio nuts over the pastry, followed by a third of the remaining confectioners' sugar and a third of the remaining lemon zest. Lay another piece of filo over the top and repeat with the butter, nuts, sugar, and zest. Repeat the process once more and finish with the fourth layer of pastry on top.

5 Cut the pastry into quarters and arrange them in four little cups in a muffin pan. Brush the pastry with the remaining melted butter.

6 Cook in the middle of the oven for 10 minutes, or until crisp and golden. Remove from the oven and leave the tart shells in the pan to cool.

7 Carefully lift out the four cooled tart shells and place on a serving plate. Divide the crème fraîche equally between the shells and arrange the strawberries on the top. Finish each with a small sprig of basil.

YOU WOULD NEVER BELIEVE IN A MILLION YEARS that this is a very healthy dessert. It is so easy to make—really quick if you prepare it for a dinner party, and your guests will be so impressed. It really can't go wrong and the flavors are amazing. If you are in need of a chocolate fix, without using real chocolate, ladies and gentlemen... I give you this.

HOT CHOCOLATE CUPS WITH PEARS & AMARETTO
Coccioli di pera e cioccolato

serves 4

177 calories   **3.9g** fat   **0.5g** saturates   **32.6g** sugars   **0.1g** salt

3 ripe pears, peeled and cored
2 tablespoons freshly squeezed lemon juice
1 tablespoon superfine sugar
1 tablespoon amaretto liqueur
⅓ cup confectioners' sugar
1 tablespoon cocoa powder
¼ cup ground almonds
1 egg white

1 Preheat the oven to 325°F.

2 Cut the pears into $^1/_2$in cubes. Place in a small saucepan with the lemon juice and superfine sugar and cook over medium heat for 12 minutes, gently stirring occasionally.

3 When they are cooked, pour the amaretto over the pears, then spoon the pears with the juices into 4 x $^1/_2$ cup ramekins.

4 To prepare the topping, sift the confectioners' sugar and the cocoa powder into a bowl. Stir in the ground almonds.

5 In a separate bowl, whisk the egg white until stiff. Gently fold the egg white into the dry ingredients.

6 Spoon the chocolate meringue mixture over the pears and shake the ramekins to level it. Bake in the middle of the oven for 20 minutes, until the topping is firm to the touch. Serve warm and enjoy!

IT MIGHT HAPPEN THAT YOU ARE HAVING GUESTS OVER FOR LUNCH/DINNER and you don't want anyone to know that you are calorie counting... this is the recipe to use. It is very luxurious, full of flavors, and yet secretly low in calories. Whatever you do, please make sure the oven is preheated before you bake the cake.

CHESTNUT & CHOCOLATE CAKE
Torta di castagne e cioccolato

serves 16

173 calories   **3.6g** fat   **1.4g** saturates   **16.9g** sugars   **0.8g** salt

1 tablespoon vegetable oil, for greasing
2 cups all-purpose flour
1 cup good-quality cocoa powder, plus extra for dusting
1 teaspoon baking powder
2 teaspoons baking soda
1¼ cups superfine sugar
pinch of salt
2 teaspoons vanilla extract
9oz chestnut purée
2 eggs
¾ cup skim milk
¾ cup cold strong coffee, preferably espresso

1 Grease a 9in cake pan with the oil (using a loose-bottomed cake pan will make your life easier) and preheat the oven to 350°F.

2 Sift the flour, cocoa powder, baking powder, and baking soda into a large bowl. Add the sugar, salt, vanilla extract, chestnut purée, and eggs. Pour in the milk and mix until well combined. Finally, mix in the coffee.

3 Pour the mixture into the cake pan and bake in the middle of the oven for about 45 minutes. To check that the cake is cooked, insert a skewer into the center: it should come out clean.

4 Leave the cake to rest for 5 minutes before turning out onto a large serving platter. Dust the top with cocoa powder and cut into 16 wedges before serving.

naughty corner

I really believe that when someone is on a diet, at some point, they will find themselves craving something that is a little bit naughty. In this chapter, the recipes I have designed have definitely got a few calories more than the others, but don't worry, just be good for the rest of the week or perhaps walk it off for 30 minutes or even have a good 20 minutes of bed action—whatever suits you best!

MANY OF YOU STILL BELIEVE THAT CARBONARA SAUCE IS MADE WITH HEAVY CREAM, bacon, and mushrooms. Well... let me tell you—this is not the way to do it. The original and traditional recipe requires only good pancetta, eggs, and cheese. Trust me—after all, I am Italian! If you can't find smoked pancetta, you can use good-quality bacon, and if you can't find Pecorino Romano, substitute it with freshly grated Parmesan cheese. It is very important for this dish that it's served immediately once it's ready, otherwise it will get pasty and dry.

PASTA WITH EGGS, PANCETTA & PECORINO ROMANO
Spaghetti alla carbonara

serves 4

610 calories   **28g** fat   **9.6g** saturates   **3.1g** sugars   **2.1g** salt

12oz spaghetti
6oz piece of smoked pancetta, rind and fat removed
2 tablespoons extra-virgin olive oil
3 eggs
¼ cup freshly grated Pecorino Romano
¼ cup finely chopped flat-leaf parsley
salt and freshly ground black pepper

1 Pour 4 quarts water into a large saucepan and bring to a boil with 3 tablespoons salt. Cook the spaghetti in the salted boiling water until al dente. To get that perfect "bite," cook the pasta for 1 minute less than instructed on the package.

2 Meanwhile, cut the pancetta into short strips about ¼in wide.

3 Heat the oil in large frying pan over medium heat. Fry the pancetta for about 5 minutes, stirring occasionally, until golden and crispy. Remove the pan from the heat and set aside.

4 Whisk the eggs in a bowl with half of the cheese. Add the parsley and plenty of black pepper.

5 Once the spaghetti is cooked, drain well, and pour into the pan with the pancetta. Pour in the egg mixture and toss together well. (The heat of the pasta will be sufficient to cook the egg for a creamy and moist texture.)

6 Season with salt and pepper and serve immediately, sprinkled with the remaining cheese.

ARTICHOKES ARE A VERY IMPORTANT VEGETABLE IN ITALY, ESPECIALLY IN THE SOUTH, where they grow in the beautiful region of Puglia. I have to admit that they are a bit tricky to prepare and that is the reason why I've used the ones from a jar in this recipe, but, of course, you can use fresh ones if you like. The combination of lamb and artichokes with a touch of white wine is absolutely wonderful. This is definitely a dish that can be used as a main course for dining al fresco with your friends or family. Make sure you buy the jarred artichokes in oil and not in water, because they will stay tender and the flavor is much better.

LAMB CUTLETS WITH ARTICHOKES & MINT
Costolette di agnello alla menta

serves 4

750 calories   **45.6g** fat   **12.3g** saturates   **2.8g** sugars   **2.2g** salt

2 tablespoons extra-virgin
   olive oil
2 garlic cloves, crushed
1 x 14.5oz jar of artichoke
   hearts in oil, drained
   and halved
2 tablespoons rosemary leaves
1¾lbs lamb cutlets, fat removed
salt and freshly ground
   black pepper
¼ cup white wine
10 mint leaves, finely chopped
1 ciabatta loaf

1 Heat the oil in a large frying pan and fry the garlic until it starts to sizzle.

2 Add the artichokes, rosemary, and the lamb cutlets and cook over medium heat for 1 minute, then turn the cutlets and cook for another minute.

3 Season with salt and pepper, pour in the wine, sprinkle in the mint, and continue to cook for 3 minutes, turning the meat over again halfway through.

4 When the cutlets are ready, place them in the middle of a large serving dish, arrange the artichokes around it, and pour the juices from the pan over the top. Serve hot with the bread cut into 8 slices.

THERE IS NO WAY THAT I WOULD HAVE WRITTEN AN ITALIAN COOKBOOK without using one of my favorite pasta dishes. If you need to, you can prepare the lasagne 24 hours before cooking it in this recipe and once it's cooked it will last in the fridge for a good 48 hours.

BAKED PASTA WITH GROUND BEEF & BÉCHAMEL SAUCE
Lasagne

serves 6

562 calories   **34.3g** fat   **17.9g** saturates   **15.2g** sugars   **1.3g** salt

2 tablespoons olive oil
1 onion, finely chopped
1 large carrot, peeled and
   finely chopped
1 celery stick, finely chopped
1lb extra-lean ground beef
salt and freshly ground
   black pepper
½ cup dry red wine
1 x 14.5oz can chopped tomatoes
1 tablespoon tomato paste
1 zucchini, finely chopped
10 basil leaves
9 fresh lasagne sheets, each
   about 4 x 7in
½ cup freshly grated Parmesan
5 tablespoons cold butter, cut
   into small cubes

for the béchamel sauce
7 tablespoons butter
½ cup all-purpose flour
1 quart cold skim milk
⅓ cup freshly grated Parmesan
½ teaspoon freshly grated
   nutmeg

1   Heat the olive oil in a large saucepan over medium heat and cook the onion, carrot, and celery for 5 minutes, stirring occasionally. Add the ground beef and continue to cook for another 5 minutes, stirring continuously, until browned. Season with salt and pepper and cook for another 5 minutes, stirring occasionally.

2   Stir in the wine and continue to cook for 3 minutes to evaporate the wine. Add the chopped tomatoes, tomato paste, zucchini, and basil. Lower the heat and continue to cook for 1 hour, uncovered, until you get a beautiful rich sauce. Stir occasionally and after 30 minutes taste for seasoning.

3   Meanwhile, make the béchamel sauce. Melt the butter in a large saucepan over medium heat. Stir in the flour and cook for 1 minute. Gradually whisk in the cold milk, lower the heat, and cook for 10 minutes, whisking constantly. Once the sauce has thickened, stir in the Parmesan with the nutmeg, season with salt and pepper, and set aside to cool slightly. Preheat the oven to 350°F.

4   Spread a quarter of the béchamel sauce on the bottom of a deep 2-quart oven-proof dish. Lay 3 lasagne sheets on top, cutting them, if necessary, to fit the dish. Spread half of the meat sauce over, then top with a third of the remaining béchamel sauce. Lay 3 more sheets of lasagne on top and cover with the remaining meat sauce. Spread over half the remaining béchamel sauce. Add a final layer of lasagne sheets and gently spread the rest of the béchamel on top, ensuring that you completely cover the lasagne sheets. Sprinkle with the Parmesan and scatter the cubed butter over the top. Grind some black pepper over the whole lasagne.

5   Cook in the bottom of the oven for 30 minutes, then transfer to the middle shelf, raise the temperature to 400°F, and continue to cook for another 15 minutes, until golden and crispy all over. Allow the lasagne to rest out of the oven for 5 minutes, then slice it and serve.

WHAT A FANTASTIC WAY TO END YOUR MEAL. To me, there is nothing better than a coffee-flavored dessert. The difference from the traditional tiramisu is that I've substituted the whipped heavy cream and mascarpone cheese with ricotta cheese and Greek yogurt—believe me when I tell you it works just as well! Make sure you dust the tiramisu with cocoa powder at the last minute just before you serve it to your guests.

RICOTTA & VANILLA TIRAMISU

Tiramisu alla ricotta

serves 8

292 calories   **14.7g** fat   **5g** saturates   **23.5g** sugars   **0.2g** salt

18oz ricotta
9oz fat-free Greek yogurt
½ cup superfine sugar
⅓ cup crushed hazelnuts
2 teaspoons vanilla extract
¾ cup cold strong coffee
½ teaspoon ground cinnamon
24 savoiardi (ladyfingers)
cocoa powder, for dusting

1   Mix the ricotta cheese with the yogurt and sugar in a large bowl. Add the hazelnuts and vanilla extract and stir until well combined.

2   Pour the cold coffee into a small bowl and mix in the cinnamon.

3   Quickly dip half the ladyfingers in the coffee and then place in the bottom of a rectangular serving dish (12 x 9in and at least 2in deep).

4   Spread half of the ricotta mixture on top. Repeat the process with the rest of the ingredients.

5   Cover the dish with plastic wrap and leave to rest in the fridge for 15 minutes.

6   Just before serving, dust the top with the cocoa powder.

WHAT AN EASY DESSERT TO MAKE—YOU REALLY CAN'T GO WRONG WITH THIS ONE. It is refreshing and tangy, yet still gives you the sweetness you want from a dessert through the crushed cookies and cinnamon. This dish is in my naughty corner but is lower in fat and calories than most cheesecakes. If you require a more lemony flavor, just add more lemon juice and zest, but make sure when you add the liquid in step 5 that it doesn't exceed a total volume of ½ cup, otherwise the cheesecake won't set properly.

LIMONCELLO & RICOTTA CHEESECAKE
Torta di ricotta e limoncello

serves 8

325 calories   **18g** fat   **10.5g** saturates   **18.5g** sugars   **0.7g** salt

2 egg whites
finely grated zest and juice
  of 2 lemons
¼ cup limoncello
1½ tablespoons granulated
  gelatin
9oz ricotta cheese
½ cup low-fat plain yogurt
5 tablespoons honey

for the base
6oz graham crackers,
  crushed
½ teaspoon ground cinnamon
6 tablespoons butter, melted
1 tablespoon butter, for
  greasing

1 To make the base, put the graham crackers, cinnamon, and melted butter in a large bowl and use your fingertips to create a mixure with the texture of wet bread crumbs.

2 Grease an 8in spring-form cake pan with the butter.

3 Press the graham cracker mixture firmly over the bottom of the pan and leave to set in the fridge for 30 minutes.

4 In a large, clean bowl, whisk the egg whites until stiff, then set aside.

5 Squeeze the lemon juice into a measuring cup or bowl, add the limoncello, and top off with enough cold water to make ¹/₂ cup. Sprinkle in the gelatin and leave to soak for 3 minutes. Place the bowl over a pan of simmering water and stir until the gelatin is dissolved. Leave to cool slightly.

6 In another bowl, whisk together the ricotta cheese, yogurt, and honey. Stir in the lemon zest and the limoncello mixture.

7 Gently fold the egg white into the mixture, pour into the pan, and level the surface. Chill for at least 5 hours, until set.

8 Remove from the pan and serve.

IN THE SUMMER OF 2009, I spent two weeks in Turkey, where cocktails were flowing all day long. This was my favorite one, especially because of all the fresh fruits that are included. If you don't have fresh berries, substitute them with some frozen ones, and instead of the mango you can use a ripe papaya. Like its title, this is a great way to start any party. Make sure that it's always served very, very cold.

PARTY PUNCH

serves 10

112 calories   **0.1g** fat   **0g** saturates   **8.1g** sugars   **0g** salt

1 x 750ml bottle very cold Italian rosé wine
2 tablespoons honey
½ cup brandy
2oz strawberries, quartered
2oz raspberries
1 mango, cut into chunks to match the size of the chopped strawberries
5 sprigs of fresh mint
2½ cups very cold sparkling water
10 ice cubes

1   Pour the wine into a large punch bowl. Stir in the honey and the brandy.

2   Add the fruit and the mint, stir everything together, and leave to rest for 10 minutes.

3   Pour in the sparkling water, add the ice, and mix.

4   To serve, ladle the punch into glasses, making sure that each serving has an ice cube and a few pieces of fruit. *Saluté*!

CONSIDERING THE FEW INGREDIENTS THAT I AM USING FOR THIS DESSERT, I guarantee you that this is going to be the easiest dish you ever prepared in your life and yet one of the tastiest. Good-quality chocolate is a must for this mousse and if raspberries are out of season, frozen ones defrosted will work in their place. Make sure you eat the mousse within 48 hours, taking into consideration that we are using fresh eggs.

LIGHT CHOCOLATE MOUSSE WITH RASPBERRIES & ORANGE ZEST
Coppette di cioccolato

serves 6

240 calories **13.9g** fat **6.9g** saturates **22.8g** sugars **0.1g** salt

7oz good-quality dark chocolate, chopped
4 eggs
grated zest and juice of 1 orange
7oz raspberries

1 Melt the chocolate in a heat-proof bowl over a pan of simmering water, ensuring that the base of the bowl does not touch the water. Set aside to cool but not to harden.

2 Meanwhile, separate the egg yolks from the whites and place in two dry, clean bowls.

3 Whisk the egg whites until stiff.

4 Beat the egg yolks together with all the juice and half the zest of the orange for 2 minutes.

5 Use a metal spoon to fold the melted chocolate gently into the egg yolk mixture a little at a time. Finally, fold in the egg whites, gently mixing all the ingredients together.

6 Divide the raspberries between six dessert glasses, reserving a few or decoration.

7 Pour the chocolate mixture over the raspberries and cover with plastic wrap. Leave to rest in the fridge for 3 hours, until set.

8 Just before serving, remove the plastic wrap and decorate the mousses with the reserved raspberries and some of the remaining orange zest.

INDEX